D1741669

The Other Side

Becoming Limitless
Through Spirit, Mind and Body
MASTERY

Dan Ginzburg

The Other Side
Becoming Limitless Through Spirit, Mind and Body Mastery

Copyright © 2021 by Dan Ginzburg

RHG Media Productions
25495 Southwick Drive #103
Hayward, CA 94544.

Paperback ISBN: 978-1-7372525-0-4
Hardcover ISBN: 978-1-7372525-1-1

Visit us online at www.YourPurposeDrivenPractice.com

Printed in the United States of America.

What People Are Saying

"Dan has many nuggets of wisdom in his book and he walks gracefully hand-in-hand with the reader as he presents them."

– Jean Walters, best-selling author

"Expansion and conscious mastery start on the first page of this book!"

– Maricruz P. Ibarra, BA. psychology & applied research

"I highly recommend this book for anyone looking to be eternally happy, independently of anything or anyone."

– Catherine Laub, keynote speaker, author, and podcaster

Dedication

This book is dedicated to every single person seeking spirit, mind, body mastery.

Acknowledgments

I love my grandpa, Nikolay Vasilevich Ponomarev. He is the one who always told me to be a well-rounded person. When I grew up, I did everything to help him with his spirit, mind, and body mastery. It was a true blessing. Giving to the person who gave you the most when you were little. I wanted him to feel like he was getting a full return on all that he invested in me. That man is a true inspiration and without his positive outlook on life, I wouldn't have mine. Moreover, there wouldn't be me, but that's another story.

Table of Contents

Preface

Hello, my dear friend. I have a burning desire to show you this. This is not a spiritual personal development book, it is a guide to a balanced living, where you effortlessly flow to your dreams and desires while exploring infinite happiness. When you're balanced and flowing, happiness, money, health, wealth, youth, relationships, love and success all become attainable to you with ease. It's not about doing more, but rather less. You may exclaim, "That's impossible!" And I say, "Welcome, to *The Other Side,* where the impossible becomes possible."

I may be wrong, but I feel like humanity needs this book right now. If you say, "Well, we survived just fine since the ice age, why now? The ice age might have been a little rough, and our history in general was very unforgiving, but what we are facing right now is not normal. It is extraordinary.

Right now, right at this moment, we are being exposed to more information than ever before. It is truly a phenomenon. We live in the age of knowing anything and knowing nothing; we may feel connected to everybody and be disconnected from everyone; we may feel like we know ourselves but have no idea who we are. While all of this doesn't help us deal with life, this book does.

Expectations are important, and I understand that your time is valuable. Here is what you can expect from this book: since 2009 I have been collecting lessons taught by the most influential people of the 21st century: spiritual leaders that shaped history and the most successful individuals of the world. This content is extracted from over fifty books in spiritual and personal development, numerous courses, and over hundreds of videos from leading self-advancement influencers. I compiled everything into a tightly packed piece of work treated by my own realizations and tested by my clients who I've mentored and consulted over the years. I also included insights that helped me get through tough times in my own human experience in the hopes that you can relate.

My grandpa used to always tell me that I have to be a well-rounded person. This became my way of life, which continues to help me live balanced. This book is therefore a very elaborate representation of my grandpa's influence on my identity. The next 180 pages incorporate practical spirituality, quantum physics, psychology, philosophy, and science to deliver to you a different category of personal development.

The structure of this book is simple. There are three parts: spirit, mind and body. Everything in those parts is written to help you accomplish two things: **to let go of everything preventing you from *ascending* and to have a clear understanding of HOW to be eternally happy, independently of anything or anyone.**

The good news is you don't have to undergo intense training, do lots of work, change yourself, your place of living, your friend circle, job, hobbies, or anything else except for one thing—your perspective. All I do is invite you to see the other side.

I don't need much. If you derive at least one thing from this book that will create a positive shift in you, my life mission will be that much closer to being accomplished. I wrote this book not because I wanted to positively influence the world; I am too small and insignificant for that. I wrote this book to positively influence just YOUR world, my friend.

You picked up this book for a reason and it is probably because you want to self-improve. If you have a desire for that, you are already doing great! Don't let anyone tell you otherwise. But why not do better? Why not be limitless?

Part I

SPIRIT

Chapter 1

A Life of a Spiritual Being

You don't have to be religious to be spiritual. If you are religious that is great, but that is not what this book is inclined toward. This book is about practical spirituality and how it can help you excel in this busy, competitive world. I personally recognize and study all religions. I agree with some ideas of each one, and I find it fascinating to discover the reasons why people believe what they believe.

I was raised to believe in God, but around the age of fourteen, I lost my faith. When I was twenty-six, I stepped back on the path. However, this time I called it the Universe.

Some people reading this book may not consider themselves spiritual or religious, and that is okay. Sometimes, pure knowledge can take you very far. I do think that people who do not at least believe in some power greater than themselves have a harder time broadening their perspective beyond the world they were conditioned to see. Ultimately, there are lots of benefits of being spiritual. The biggest one is becoming less affected by the hardships of our human experience that may paralyze our growth and advancement.

In the Western culture, people usually refer to balanced living as the development of mind, body, spirit. However, I truly believe that it is spirit, mind, body. Spiritual advancement has to always come first; without it, the building blocks of the mind that are supposed to support the body will not stand. Why? Because without spirituality, we are extremely vulnerable. We live in the confinements of our EGO, which stands for earthly guide only.

Guided by earthly values, we may fall into a false belief that we own the house we live in, the car we drive, the money we have, our friends, relatives, pets, and everything else. You don't own any of it! At any moment, all of that can be taken away from you.

In the matter of a day, the stock market may crash, your house burn down, your car stolen, and everyone you know die from some virus. I know this sounds negative, but these are just mere examples. Then what? What will happen to you? Do you see how fragile and vulnerable thinking that we own all of that makes us?

You don't even own your own body, because you may have some freak accident on the way to work, and now you are paralyzed forever. Even your mind you don't own, because you can have a stroke or Alzheimer's, and then what? All of that can be taken away from you.

The only thing we truly own is our spirit, our soul, our energy, our consciousness. That is us. THAT is something no one can take away from us. So, doesn't it make the most sense to spend the most time cultivating that what we truly own? Yet, so many people give so little focus to their spirituality.

When we realize that everything else can be taken away from us, that is when the magical detachment from everything that is not us begins. That is when we become much less affected by the hardships of our human experience.

I always wondered about those people who transformed the minute they crossed the lavish doorways of their churches. It's as if at the entrance there was this illusory "behave differently now that you're here" check-in. They sort of took off the mask behind which there was this kind, empathetic person who believed in God. Or perhaps, they put one on. When they returned to the world outside of church grounds, they no longer saw themselves as seeking spiritual experience and so they reverted back to their regular selves — a bit judgmental, doubtful, maybe selfish. I thought to myself, "Church is really good for them."

I saw that many people try to become spiritual by engaging in certain activities, such as going to church or celebrating religious holidays. As much as they try, they are missing the bigger picture. To them, spirituality is an experience that they seek, but it is quite the opposite, actually. Paramahansa Yogananda, one of the greatest Yogis and a guru who brought the concept of self-realization to the West, said, **"We are not human beings seeking a spiritual experience, we are spiritual beings having a human experience."**

Spirituality is about regaining touch with our true inner self — our consciousness. That self that has not been polluted and swayed by all of the controversies of our world. At our birth, our spirituality is very strong, our intuition is very pure, and our consciousness is very clear because we have not been separated from our true spiritual nature by our human experience yet. In the *Gospel of Thomas*, it even says, "The man old in days will not hesitate to ask a small child seven days old about the place of life, and he will live."[1] We can learn a lot from children.

As you can see, being spiritual is not an experience, it is a way of being. Meanwhile, experiencing life on this earth separates us from it, if we let it. This partially explains why the church is so transformative for some folks. When they are in it, they detach themselves from the everyday life struggles.

I don't blame them. The human experience can get in the way. It is full of problems, obligations, making money, upholding a certain image, judgment, jealousy, competition or even betrayal. Many people really bend down to their human experience, unfortunately, and I used to be one of those people for many years.

It's not easy, let's face it, and so some allow their hardships to anger them, hurt them, to turn them away from their loved ones. Others let everyday obstacles ruin their health because they find great meaning in their problems. Many deal with the pain by countering it with bodily pleasures, such as: delicious food, sex, consumerism, drugs, dopamine … until they crash.

---

[1] Lambdin (trans.), *Gospel of Thomas*, verse 4, p. 1.

It's understandable, we all want to be happy. So, some people chase after these glimpses of meaningless, immediate happiness, and for some time it works. However, the pain re-occurs — because it never goes away, it just takes a back seat, from where it navigates their lives. It tells them what turn to take where, and what stop to make when. That is what makes us lose touch with our natural spiritual self.

To regain that contact, we have to realize that this is not who we are. We are not stressed out, we experience stress; we are not angry, we experience anger; we are not regretful, we experience regret; we are not depressed, we experience depression.

We are spiritual beings and this whole thing called life is just is simply happening to us; it is not us, it is not even part of us. The only thing that is us is our soul, our energy, our consciousness, and our spirit. Which, by the way, you will see all used synonymously here. That is why the quintessence of spirituality, is connecting with our true self.

Meanwhile, the human experience is very persistent in trying to detach us from our true selves. It tries every day, which is why we can never give in; we have to consciously try to remain unaffected by it.

Our human experience derives from our environment, and so instinctively, the best solution to this is to get away from it. Interestingly enough, this is exactly why monks or holy people who are able to achieve the extraordinary, tend to live in the monasteries or mountains or somewhere away from society.

Imagine how much energy they save by not having to deal with everyday struggles. The amount of undivided concentration that they can give to their spiritual advancement. Having that much focused energy is what allows them to achieve higher consciousness and true divinity within. However, they are still people just like us.

That is what is so fascinating — we ALL have that capacity! Unfortunately, not all of us have the opportunity to leave civilization and enjoy life without earthly difficulties. Our life will go on, we cannot completely eliminate our environment. **We can only change how we respond to it.** The more energy we conserve, the more we will have to use for our spiritual success, and the more spiritually successful we are, the more effective we will be in our earthly accomplishments such as our financial, physical, and societal situations.

How do we know if we are becoming more spiritual?

Five things will start happening:

1. You will start seeing beauty in ordinary things
2. Your intuition will get stronger
3. Your emotional self-awareness will increase
4. You will get excited more, even about simple things
5. You will be calmer and less emotionally affected by hardships

Spiritual Prosperity

Spiritual prosperity lies in being in tune with the Universe. Being in tune with the Universe lies in being in touch with your spirit. Being in touch with your spirit is accomplished by raising our vibrations, and for that, we have to experience fewer negative emotions. Doubt, regret, hatred, stress, anger, fear, and dozens more are all negative emotions that lower our vibrations. In this book, we learn how to change our perspective to minimize experiencing those negative emotions.

The Universe is always guiding us. When we are in tune, we understand that guidance very clearly.

I really learned a lot from Paramahansa Yogananda. His teachings helped me to discover self-realization. One thing that he said that really moved me was that, "If we first develop spiritual magnetism, it would guide us in the proper ways to supply all of our natural needs." What is spiritual magnetism, and why is it important?

Magnetism means energy, because we attract with energy. What this saying above really means is that it is not exactly the spiritual magnetism that guides us. Rather it allows us to attract that what we want.

Negativity is what weakens our spiritual magnetism, and so it is no longer able to guide us toward success, or at the very least, our natural needs. By cleaning our energy, we remove the blockages that separate us from being in harmony with the Universe and so receive its guidance. Now, when we are in harmony, everything else starts to fall into place.

If we free ourselves from all of the obstructions, the skies will open and listen to our needs and desires. If we have our magnetism polluted by the earthly vices, the connection between us and the Universe is weak and interrupted.

Similarly, in life, we have to trust the Universe to take us where we need to be, because ultimately, we are in the darkness of the unknown. We have no idea what will happen tomorrow. Yet, we cannot have any disturbances that will weaken the touch of the powerful hand when it reaches to take us where we need to be.

The path to prosperity is a straight path, but we are the ones who place the rocks in our way, dig holes in the ground, construct impossible walls to climb, and lay mines in the soil. If we cleanse our energy of all negativity, we will clear our path. And the Universe will take our hand and lead us where we want to be, with ease.

How do we do it? In the *Heart Sutra* of Mahayana Buddhism, it says, "Where your focus goes, your energy flows." When we focus on negative thoughts, we feed them with energy. The common saying, "Oh, just don't think about that," goes far beyond the simple advice of not getting upset or stressed out about something. The more we focus on our spirit, and not the negativity generated by our mind and body, the faster we will strengthen our spiritual magnetism and our connection to the source, the Universe.

This may be hard at first, but through increased self-awareness and mindfulness, it is very possible. Repetition is the mother of all learning. When you will finally start operating from your spirit is when you will start noticing a difference in how you feel. That is how you will know that you are on the path of spiritual prosperity. Soon thereafter, you will realize how limitless you can be, and that is when you will begin to discover the divinity within.

Chapter 2

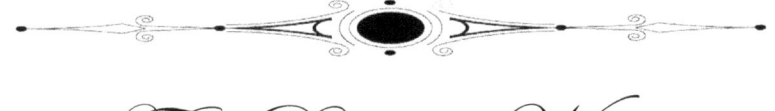

The Divinity Within

Many religions are a path to God. This is why most of the religious literature has many underlining principles in common. When I say God, I mean whatever you believe in: the Holy Father, the Lord, the Yahweh, or the Braham. Whatever it is, have you ever seen Them in person? I certainly have not. Yogis have learned that God can never be found outside themselves. This is very contrary to many religions because they portray God as a third-person figure that is physically present somewhere out there.

After visiting the Louvre, the Vatican, the Hermitage and the Prado Museum of Art, I found something strikingly similar between all of them. It was how many paintings depicted God. I inquired into the reason behind that. It turned out that through art, people learned to believe in God. Artists such as Michelangelo, Leonardo, and many others realized that it is very hard to believe in something you can't see or imagine. So, they illustrated God, to help people believe in Him.

The truth is, you will never meet God like those people in Michelangelo's and Leonardo's famous paintings. God comes from your belief in Him. Think about it, to those who don't believe in God, He doesn't exist, not here, not in the sky, not anywhere. Therefore, God really exists in our belief in Him, and where does our belief come from? This is why God is within you, which is where the phrase, "The Divinity within," originates from.

However, that phrase carries a very empowering meaning. When I studied at the Self-Realization Fellowship Shrine in Malibu, California, during our mediation sessions, we always said, "Reveal Thyself." For a long time, I could not understand what it was that I was supposed to see. Was I looking for God to reveal his image to me? Was I supposed to feel something? Hear something? For months, I was clueless.

Every time I asked someone from our group about it, I got these vague answers that didn't mean anything to me at that time. After months of meditation and absolute confusion, there was a moment when I finally realized what that phrase meant. Yet it happened at the most unexpected moment, definitely not during meditation.

When I was studying for the California Bar exam to become a lawyer, it took a tremendous amount of willpower to stay consistent with my preparation. A perfect day was when I woke up at seven in the morning and studied until ten at night, with one two-hour break in between at two o'clock. At first, I could not force myself to even do half of that regimen. I had never had to do anything that required this much discipline. It seemed impossible to me to do even just do two practice essays and twenty multiple-choice questions.

After struggling for a whole month, one day I finally had a breakthrough. In one day, I did three essay questions and thirty-two multiple-choice questions. The next day, I did three essay questions and seventy multiple-choice questions! More than triple what I started out with.

I remember at the end of the last question, I closed my computer, leaned back in my chair, looked into the ceiling and said to myself, "That's unreal." If somebody would have told me a month earlier that I would be able to concentrate for this long and endure that much testing, I would have never believed them. It just would have seemed unattainable, because it would have required so much power of will.

That was the moment when I realized that the one thing that distinguishes those who can accomplish the extraordinary from all others, is **the power of will**! That day I did the most questions and my willpower was at its all-time high. That was when I realized what that phrase "Revel Thyself" meant to me.

It meant to feel the power of God inside of yourself. This is where people that believe that God created us have a bit of an advantage over those who don't. If God created us, that means that He is our father and so part of his power is in us. I personally associate with this belief, and I can't say that it is religiously motivated. It just gives me a feeling like I can do anything, and that is a pretty resourceful feeling to have in our modern, competitive world.

God's power is felt through our power of will. Think what would change in you if you realized that part of God's power is within you. How would you approach your wishes, knowing that your willpower is not human, not earthly, but divine? Your power of will is the power of God. We all have it, but not all realize it, and even less, use it.

All of those people who set world records, people who can memorize four decks of cards, monks who crushed twenty-seven piled bricks with their fist, or Kung Fu masters who chopped down bamboo trees with their bare feet. It seems like they have some kind of a gift, something superhuman.

However, they are all people just like us. The one way they are different is that they exercise their divine willpower more often. Doing a one-arm, one-finger pushup seems like something that would require unhuman abilities. In reality, it just takes six years of consistent training.

Now, let's take it a step further, what about people who can heal others? I studied reiki just out of curiosity, and I realized that the reason I can't heal anyone is because I need to put in one year of training before I could even think about healing another person. Although before reiki became more mainstream, it was thought that only a saint or Jesus could heal another person.

How about people who transcend their human bodies, and enter astral projection, where the soul leaves the body controllably? I actually met a Shaman who could do that. He said after he experienced it, he no longer feared death. I asked him how long did it take him to do that? I thought he was going to give me some shamanic answer, like he was born with this ability because he learned it in his past life or something.

His answer was actually very realistic. He said it took him about four years of meditating every single day. It was a strange moment for me when I heard that. Before his answer, he was half human-half God to me, but after, he became just a regular person that did what anybody could do, if they were disciplined.

One of the meanings of self-realization is realizing the power of God within you. With this power, we can not only achieve extraordinary physical abilities or great financial success, we can accomplish astonishing happiness, but it will take self-control.

Yet don't let that discourage you, it is all just part of life. Without discipline, dreams cannot turn into goals, and goals cannot turn into accomplishments. What matters is that we are all born with unearthly willpower. It is in us! Right now, as you read this, you have this all-powerful, divine, limitless willpower. It is pulsating inside of you. All you have to do is let it reveal thyself.

Let God Work Trough You

I remember this was another phrase I could not understand for a long time. I thought it meant to let God guide you through life, or to trust God to let things that were meant to be, happen to you. It turned out to be something completely different.

Sometimes when you help another person, that person says "Thank God," but he really is thanking you. In a way, it can be perceived as if God has used your hands to help that person, He has worked through you.

I agree with some things Tony Robbins says, and disagree with others. One thing that he said that truly moved me is that before he gets on stage, he says, "God, use me." I wonder how many people that Tony helped during their tough times said, "Thank God for that experience."

Again, you don't have to be religious or believe in God to enjoy the benefits of this concept. Just realize that what we put out into this world, is what we receive back. When you know this, the whole world will be at your command.

The more love and kindness we put out, the more comes back to us. I learned this the most from my mother, Nataly. She always had this unconditional love for people in this world. My mom truly served others in her life, and sometimes even strangers, every chance she got. She let God work through her. In return, she was and continues to be rewarded with incredible youth, happiness, and energy.

A single person has the capacity to change masses. Once you will feel God's energy flowing through you, and your wishes coincide with God's desires, you will become more powerful than ever, and your willpower will begin being unearthly.

The more love we spread, the less hate we have in our hearts; the more kindness we give, the less negativity will be in us; the more empathy we share, the more loving this world will appear to us. Our strength does not have to be obtained; it can be merely realized. It is already inside of us, but to use it we have to channel it properly. Remember, the measure of your life is not in duration, but in donation.

Lastly, spiritual success is the highest form of success.

Chapter 3

The Energy

Our human experience can be very complex. We may be seeking spiritual success, we may deal with personal problems, experiencing great hardship, identifying our purpose, and figuring out where we fit in this world. Regardless of all of these complexities, I always found it fascinating how simple our life model really is.

If you think about it, the reason why we try to find our purpose, seek spiritual success, work hard, make money, spend money, get into relationships, have kids, move to other countries, meditate, medicate, work out, go out, stay out, is all to be happy. Every single thing we do, every single action we take in life, if we deconstruct it, it will all lead to our ultimate motive, to be happy.

Let's take something that may seem completely unrelated, paying child support. One having such obligation may absolutely hate it and do it because they have to, pursuant to court order. However, they do it, because if they don't, they would have to face legal consequences that would make them a lot more unhappy than putting up with this monthly expense. Engaging in a burdensome activity to avoid greater suffering is done for what? To preserve happiness. So, in a way, that person is paying child support to be happy.

Even if we take the most selfless act, such as taking care of others or donating to a charity, we do it because it makes us feel good, which makes us happy. Regardless of whether all of those things will actually make us happy, our underlying, subconscious motive is our own happiness. All roads lead to one place.

The bigger question, however, is what is it about happiness that makes us pursue it endlessly our entire life? Perhaps it is because when we are happy, we feel alive, uninhibited and excited. We are electric, we want to try new things, visit new places, and conquer new heights. The dopamine centers of our brain are firing, and our serotonin levels are high, giving us confidence and a feeling like we can do it all.

All of these states of being can be summarized by one word – ENERGY. Happiness gives us energy. Our whole life is a constant pursuit of happiness because it really is an ongoing battle for energy. All comes down to it. **The more energy we have, the more resourceful we are, the more we can do, and the more we can be.** This is why monks and many holy people live away from the civilization, to not waste their energy on earthly struggles, and instead use it to accomplish limitlessness.

What astonishes me, however, is how much of our energy we do indeed waste, after working so hard for it. What is interesting, is how much of it is wasted on self-sabotage.

The reason why many people are not remarkably happy is not because they lack something or someone. It is because of their inability to deal with suffering. In the process of attempting to deal with it, they sabotage themselves, and ultimately their happiness.

Notice that although the source of suffering is our human experience, it is not what drains our energy. Many people may disagree with me because they believe that it is their job, their boss, their partner, or something else external that is taking away their energy by causing them to suffer.

Those people say things like: "My job stresses me out, my husband makes me angry, the exam makes me fearful, I will regret this for the rest of life" or "I doubt I will ever make it." It is true that suffering results from many negative emotions, and the five big ones are indeed stress, anger, fear, regret, and doubt.

However, do realize that those emotions derive from our *reactions* to the human experience, not the human experience itself. Our reaction to the job, the boss, the partner, or the exam. Where do those reactions come from? No other place but US! Not the environment.

Nobody is forcing us to react the way we do. Thus, we are ultimately the ones causing ourselves to suffer. We are in control, and if we are in control then **we have a choice not to waste our energy on our human experience.**

To do that, however, we have to master dealing with stress, anger, fear, regret, and doubt. If we don't, we will never break the cycle of wasting energy on negative emotions and attracting events that make us experience more of them.

By the way, I don't personally believe there are "negative" or "positive" emotions, I think they are all just emotions. There are ones of low vibrational frequencies, like the ones we mentioned above, and there are others of high vibrational frequencies, such as joy, love, gratitude, appreciation, excitement, and many more. I will refer to them as positive and negative just because it is shorter and less confusing.

Magnetism

Have you ever had a day that starts bad, and then only gets worse? I used to have days like that. It usually happened to me in the kitchen while getting ready in the morning. I would either drop something or spill something, and of course, I would get really mad. I couldn't understand why all the subsequent shit had to happen though.

It felt as if by reacting with anger, I was attracting another event to be angry about. This feeling became backed up by facts. I began to notice this in other areas of my life. When I would experience road rage, more awful drivers would somehow be sent my way for me to get enraged about; when I would get mad at someone, magically, I would have more encounters with people that would make me mad; when I would have problems at work and would react to them emotionally, more problems at work would find me. It just wouldn't stop. I wasted so much energy on all of this.

This went on for years, until one day when I had an occasional coffee accident at six in the morning. I remember it vividly. I turned around too quickly and the side of my hand caught the edge of my favorite mug. I watched that mug and the fresh, black coffee in it leaving the countertop, becoming air borne, undoubtedly heading in the direction of my perfectly clean khaki pants, and so it happened, again. I watched all of it in slow motion. My heart skipped a beat as I was getting ready to massacre everything. I already looked at the cabinet I was going to punch, but then I thought to myself, "I can't have a fucked-up day today."

In that moment, I decided that this has to end, and the only way was for me to not start it. I paused, took a deep breath, looked up and told myself, "It's okay, this will not ruin my day, not today." I quietly took off my hopelessly stained pants, put them in the sink and put on new ones, black ones, just in case.

Now my outfit didn't match. But I once again took a deep breath and said, "It's okay, this will not ruin my day, not today." The rest of the day went fine. My theory was proved.

How can we explain this? We are magnetically changed with energy, and so we have the ability to attract. We attract energy that comes in the forms of events, people, and circumstances because everything is made out of energy. When we charge our magnetism with negative energy, we then attract more events that match that energy. This is why negative people are not very lucky, they always have some shit happen to them.

Stress attracts stress, negative attracts negative, anger attracts anger. We are magnetic. I will explain how this works on a biological and quantum physical level later in the book. For now, just know that to avoid attracting this kind of negativity, we have to not react to the hardships of our human experience negatively in the first place. **We must strive to respond with calmness,** instead. When we have clean magnetism, or spiritual magnetism as we refer to it in Chapter One, we will attract that what we want more of, and NOT that what makes us stressed, angry, or dissatisfied.

What We Put Out is What We Put In

I recently bought a juicer, because I was enthusiastic about making carrot-mango-lemon punch. I noticed that every single time I squeezed a mango, mango juice came out. Every time I squeezed a lemon, lemon juice came out. Every time I squeezed a carrot, carrot juice came out. This happened every single time. Not once did I squeeze a mango and have lemon juice come out.

We are the same way, whatever we have inside of us, that is what comes out when we are squeezed. If we have anger and hate inside of us, when we are triggered, happiness and love are not going to come out. You might have come across people like that. They are either always angry or always pissed off about something.

You also might have met people who appear to be social and outgoing, but when something squeezes them, rage comes out. How come? Why does this happen? People like that will always be energy-depleted because they waste so much of it on negative emotions. In addition, their magnetism is not clean, and so it cannot guide them to where they want to be. The question is, how do those emotions that come out, get in?

If we have an unfavorable event happen and we react to it by blowing up with anger, guess what we just did? We put anger inside of us. Now, the next time someone does something not very thoughtful and we are squeezed, we will spill out anger. **What we put out is what we put in, through our reaction to our human experience**.

This can become a vicious cycle of endless energy deprivation. If one reacts with stress, one puts more stress inside of themselves. As a result, next time they react with more stress, and this can go on for years. Some people are what they say, chronically stressed out for this very reason. In addition, this can lead to serious health issues, discussed in the next chapter, and even character can change over time. This is why we must either break the cycle, or never get trapped in it in the first place. And now the biggest question of all, how?

It will be answered in great detail in Chapter Five, but for now, I would like to offer you a more all-embracing, predominant solution to help you conserve as much of your energy as possible.

Chapter 4

Is the Universe Perfect?

Have you ever had something happen that made you ask, "What have I done to deserve this?" It could be some unfavorable event that leaves us with a heavy feeling, or sometimes just something one said.

In Buddhism, one of the main underlying principles is that nothing in this life is permanent. We are born and we die, the rainbow comes and it fades, the snow falls and it melts, nothing is forever. A good feeling will never last indefinitely; it will eventually pass, and so will a bad one.

However, some of us don't let it pass. We latch on to it. Sometimes for days, sometimes for weeks, or even years. We drown in regret of not taking a different course of action, we imagine how things would have been but for this one thing we did. We waste enormous amounts of energy on it, screaming how this is all not fair, how it is not right. We let it destroy us.

So then, how do we improve the skill of letting the negative go? How do we leave it behind? The answer lies in our understanding of where our attachment to our past comes from. It stems from us having this idea that things could have been otherwise and that we should have done something differently. Here are two things I invite you to realize, my friend, and forever **allow** to serve you:

"There is NOTHING **that could have been otherwise."**

"There is NOTHING **that you should have done differently."**

Nothing that happened to you up to this point in your life was on accident. Imagine that the Universe makes no mistake. By Universe, I mean whatever you believe in that is bigger than you. It can be God, Allah, the Holly Spirit, or just the field of energy that is proven to exist by quantum physics, which we will talk about later.

If we believe that the Universe will always act in our favor and it will never do things to hurt us, we can be free from latching on to our past, deteriorating our present. In the moment when awful things happen to us, we may believe the exact opposite. How can an injury, going to jail, losing millions, or losing someone, be done not to hurt us? Of course, this all hurts us!

But no, an injury could be sent to us as an opportunity to strengthen other parts of our body and our power of will; going to jail could gift us with an enormous amount of time to rethink our lives and not make bigger mistakes, losing millions can humble us and help us appreciate more, losing someone can teach us about how important it is to be present, enjoy every moment and for us to teach that to others in need.

When you throw a rock in a lake, it creates splashes and waves, but nature has a way to restore the peace, and soon the lake comes back to its motionless, beautiful state. The Universe is the same way, it tries to restore our peace in every way it can.

The faster we learn to trust the divine intelligence, the faster we can let go of the unfavorable past and emotions associated with it. If it happened, it was on purpose and that's the end of it, because now it is out of our reach, it is in the past. So, in a way, contemplating it is meaningless. What are you going to do if you believe it was unjust or unfair? Will you build a time machine? What is in our reach however, is our present and that is the only place where our focus should be.

The present needs us. If we had something happen that carried detrimental consequences, we now need to resolve them. To do so in the fastest most effective manner, we need to devote as much of our energy to it as possible. However, we will not be able to do that if we waste half of our energy on trying to reverse time.

The Universe is perfect, and the reason why people are stuck in their past is because they cannot accept this simple idea. They fight their past, they disagree with it, and so they don't let it do its natural thing, they don't let it pass. It wants to, but they hold on to it, replaying it, letting it ruin their present and certainty their future.

The Practical Approach

It is not about having this blind belief that everything happens for a reason. Believing that the Universe is perfect is a philosophy of self-preservation. The faster we accept, the less resistance we create in allowing the improvement to happen. Think about it, the more time we spend drowning in the negative emotions associated with our problems, the worse we feel. The more we think about the problem rather than its solution, the more negative emotions we experience. Moreover, the more misfortune we attract. **Where our attention goes our energy flows, and where our energy flows the more of that we end up with in our life.**

Why do we do that? Because we fail to realize that this hardship was sent to us for a reason. The Universe made no mistake. The faster we accept that, the faster we can move on and the better we will feel. We may never find out the reason, and frankly, it doesn't matter. It only matters to our EGO.

We cannot give our time to the unwanted, feed it with our energy and attention, and then end up with the wanted. As long as we focus on the injustice, unfairness, or the unwanted, we align ourselves with the vibrations of the unjust, unfair, and unwanted and simply attract more of it.

This is why it is impossible to create an improved future by focusing on the unfortunate past. The fastest way to move to a new, improved situation is to make peace with your current one, ONLY then can we stop resisting the improvements that are waiting for us. This is why we must focus on what we should do right now, rather than kicking ourselves about what we should have done yesterday. Yesterday is long gone.

Our focus is very powerful, it is charged with energy and our energy is what attracts events, circumstances, and people into our life. The more we focus on something, the stronger its vibrational frequency becomes and the more of it we see show up in our life. So, if we constantly focus on our problem, the problem becomes a stronger vibration than the solution, and then we wonder when will we get a break from all these difficulties.

You might have seen this in people who continuously complain about all the shit in their life, and the more they complain, the more shit happens to them. This is why. **We cannot find the solution to a problem when the problem is the stronger vibration**. It will always overpower any solution, and the unfortunateness will keep repeating or just never end.

Understand this, your patterns of thought do not have to follow your current situation. No matter how horrible your current situation may be, you do not have to focus all of your energy and attention on how bad you feel about it. You have a choice to shift your attention. The faster you realize that there is nothing you should have done, and there is nothing that should have been otherwise, the easier that shift will be.

Could the Universe Ever Not Be Perfect?

As a mentor and a consultant, I worked with many people who experienced childhood trauma. I worked with girls who were sexually abused, people who were abandoned by their parents, or raised in families with serious drug abuse problems. Until I began working with folks who lived through such experiences, I had no idea how dark their worlds really were.

Here I was, this positive guy, living in the name of light, being dropped into the depth of a dark forest that the light could not penetrate, where you hear the breaths of hundreds of hungry, wild animals, but see none at all. Where whenever you looked up, in hopes of seeing a glimpse of a blue sky, the trees got taller, and I felt I was sinking down the neurological pathways of my clients' minds. I really cared, and so to help them I had to understand them. I had to imagine being them.

What was scary is that to me this lasted for the length of our sessions, and for some time right after. For them, this was their lives. How do you tell someone who has been abused that the Universe is perfect?

I felt that the reason why my clients struggled was because they were trying to somehow solve the past. They wanted to do something about it, to change it, to correct it. They tried to find their parents to tell them how much they hate them and how they have fucked up their lives.

They wanted to make the person or the people who did this to them realize what they have done, and at least take some responsibility. I had this one girl who told me, "I sometimes want to dig up my father's grave and scream at him, just look at him and scream, so he would understand what he did." I asked her, "And what if he could somehow say, 'I'm sorry,' would that make you feel better?" She said, "It would."

I found it fascinating that many of these people were just looking for empathy. They felt like they were victims of an unfair trial that resulted in life without parole, got put away behind bars of agony and fed with hate that they digested with their hearts, and nobody cared. In their world, nothing was perfect, not just the Universe.

How can you tell them that everything that happened to them up to this point was on purpose? After a few sessions, I usually asked them, "So all your life, you were trying to make it right. What kind of results did you get?" I usually got blank stares, some started crying. I knew where their tears were coming from. It wasn't from disparity of not really accomplishing anything, it was from the realization that by battling their past, they have ruined their present. Forget about victory. One said to me, "Only if this never happened, I would have had a normal life." That phrase stuck with me for years.

Many of my clients weren't only abused in the past, they found themselves in abusive relationships in their present also. It was like they somehow attracted their past into their present. I thought about this, and realized why it was happening. By not letting it go and fighting the injustice, their attention was constantly on the traumatic events or the people who caused them. Their entire existence revolved around all this.

They talked about it endlessly, sought therapy, connected with people who went through similar experiences. I get it, they wanted to deal with it, because they felt that if it was dealt with once and for all, then the pain would just go away. Yet it didn't. It re-emerged. Every time they would tell the story, the feelings would come back up and it would feel real all over again.

They needed a permanent solution. Every time I knew what it was, every time I knew how effective it was, and every time it was so hard to say. **The quicker we forgive, the quicker we forget, and the only way to forgive is to send them love.** I tell them, "Just send them love." If that person is alive, easy, call them, see them. If they are dead, just pretend they can hear you. The moment you say those words to them, you will release yourself from this agony and hate that has been destroying you all your life. Send them love.

Having a person realize what their life was right now, why and how they came to be this way, was the moment when they would be ready to understand the value in the phrase, "The present needs you." It shifted their attention from what it was to what it is.

The magical phrase, "The Universe is perfect," would always come in the very end, after I would tell them that, "This, what you are experiencing right now, is your adult self, trying to save your young self. But those people are one person, and so I need you to just save yourself. And the way you do that is by using the awareness that your adult self has and your younger self had lacked, the ability to let go of what's already behind you. There could have been no other way, everything up to this point that has happened is on purpose, it was no mistake."

The Story of the Two Mothers

It was the end of the winter semester. The snow began to melt and the green patches of new life were emerging in the scenery of a small town in Russia. The air was softer, and the sunrays were beginning to melt the gloominess of the winter season. In Russia, the spring is a sacred time of the year that people look forward to as a new beginning, a resurrection from the cold and depressing winter.

For the kids, it is an especially wonderful time because of the spring break. In this small town, there was a school. At the last bell of the winter term, all of the children ran out joyfully breathing in their tiny little lungs the relieving feeling of freedom. To celebrate, Serge and Alex along with their eight friends, all eleven to twelve years old, went to the movie theater, located at a shopping mall.

Similarly, many other kids decided to go to the movies that day, and so the theater was flooded with this young, excited crowd. Many tried to sneak in because they didn't have the money for the ticket. To prevent this, after the show started, the employees locked the theater doors. Nobody could get in and nobody could get out.

Completely unforeseeably, a fire broke out at the shopping mall. Due to its close proximity to the movies, the flames began to quickly spread to the theater. The screen caught on fire first, and the children began to panic. They rushed to the doors, but the doors were locked. No matter how hard they tried, they could not break through them. They just weren't strong enough. They were trapped and the smoke started to suffocate everyone inside. In the end, nobody survived, including Serge and Alex.

Serge's mom, Julia, was devastated. What mother wouldn't be? She cried and shouted, "How could this be? What have I done to deserve this? What has my little boy done to end like this?!" She cried for days. She could not accept it. The world was hell and there was no God to her. She lost faith, but most of all she lost hope.

She began to drown in the darkness of depression. The light of escape began to seem smaller and smaller, further and further away. Julia resorted to medication. It helped for a while, but her dosage just could not keep up with the pain of her loss. She had to take more.

The scary moments were when she was off of the meds and one on one with herself. That was when the rotten roots of the depression extended its endings so far down her nervous system, she felt her pupils constrict. She was no longer herself; she was a bi-product of misery and chemical dependency. Yet what choice did Julia have? She had to escape the pain somehow. She began drinking, heavily.

After the inability to come to work sober for almost a month, her employer had enough; Julia got laid off. Her daily life no longer revolved around her duties as a mother to her second child, but her main duty to drugs and alcohol. As long as she had enough money to feed her addiction, the rest was secondary. Seven months later, there was nothing left of her, and her second kid's childhood was ruined.

Alex's mother, Kathryn cried and shouted just like Julia. She cried and shouted, "How could this be? What have I done to deserve this? What has my little boy done to end like this?!" This lasted a week. On the seventh day, she woke up and told herself, "The Universe makes no mistake." She wiped her tears and went to work. It was painful, but she knew that she could not bring back her boy. She had another child, a little girl. So, Katherine made a powerful decision that she will be twice the best mother and give her girl double the attention, double the love, and double the care that she would have otherwise.

Kathryn did not stop there. She started a support group for other mothers who lost their children. As a result of her own tragedy, she developed an unusual ability to empathize with others who were coping with their horrible misfortunes. She became extraordinarily effective in helping families come to terms with their losses and move on with life.

Her group received funding from the state, and soon it had hundreds of members. She gave other mothers hope. Kathryn's message was that, "We must not battle our past, because by doing that we waste the energy we need to create the future, for ourselves and those around us." Her message was powerful. It made many mothers realize that they have to maintain themselves, no matter what happens, because others need them.

May It All Be Just a Test?

There is one phrase that has helped me countlessly across the spectrum of hardship. From small things, like losing my phone or scratching my car, to big losses and tragedies. In every obstacle, lies as much opportunity as you can see. Copy the next page, or if you are listening, just write it down and put it up on your wall:

Every problem, every burden,
every difficulty, and every failure is
my opportunity to practice patience,
calmness, self-control, and to GROW
into a *relentless* human being.

What is this relentlessness measured in? In your ability to take a hit. If you can stay as unaffected as possible through tough times, you will be untouchable. The truth is, our life is not defined by our success, but rather by our ability to overcome failure. It is the divine ability to not break our focus when everything is trying to break us. That is being relentless.

I will tell you how to do that later in the book; it is just very important to mention right now. I personally don't view hardship as something that was fair or not fair, something I deserved or didn't, I view hardship as a test, a test of strength.

Some people pass, some fail. Yet the Universe makes no mistake, the divine intelligence is so clever, it knows exactly when to test you. No matter how big or small. Realize that the Universe wants you to be successful; it is not out there to ruin your life. We are the ones who can ruin our lives by not believing in this. However, to be successful you must be able to overcome suffering. Losers are not those who lose a game, they are the ones who don't get back up after they lost it.

How many times have you seen someone resort to drugs to deal with an emotional pain caused by a difficult time? With every dose, they got swallowed deeper and deeper into powerlessness. That difficult time wasn't the devil knocking on one's door, it was the Universe. The Universe whispered to one, "If you overcome this, I will reward you with strength and faith in yourself that will help you rise."

Some people experience years of repeated offerings by the Universe. They complain a lot about them. They say things like, "How much more of this do I have to take?" or "When will I get a break?" or "I hate this." Is the Universe continuously testing them? Not necessarily. That person could just be attracting the unfortunateness by complaining about it endlessly. Making the unfortunate a stronger vibration, and not allowing the improvements to take place.

Know that over time, when you fail a test, you become weaker. Every time you pass a test you become stronger. Why? Because by overcoming an obstacle, you build confidence and faith in yourself that you are capable. "If I overcame that, I can overcome this," is the phrase you will find yourself saying. The opposite is also true. "If I failed that, there is no way

I can prevail this." A person doesn't just wake up one day feeling like a failure. It is a process of repeated inability to overcome obstacles.

Think about how much Jeff Bezos, Elon Musk, and Bill Gates had to overcome to get to where they are. How many problems, how many moments when any ordinary person would fold, they fought and won. I do not know if they thought that the Universe was perfect, that every lawsuit and every loss was for a reason, but I know for sure they accepted it all as part of the journey to big success, and I know for sure every time they came out stronger.

Why is the Universe testing us? It wants us to succeed. Understand that success in life is about being able to handle the dark times. The storms will come and they will pass, but who will you be after is what determines your relentlessness.

Is There Destiny?

Do you believe in destiny? I used to believe in destiny, but I stopped. I stopped because it was too unpredictable. I would waste so much time thinking that this is what I am meant to do, this is who I am meant to be, or this is whom I am meant to be with, and I would be proved wrong every time. I thought I was going to be a lawyer full time, but then I failed my first California Bar exam.

If I had passed, I would have written this book considerably later in life, or never at all. I for sure would have never become a mentor and a consultant; I would never have had the time to create a program I now use to transform lawyers' lives and their law practices. Yet, on that day in May 2018, I was very sad. All of my plans of what I thought I was meant to do at that time went out the window. I thought that my dreams came crashing down. Little did I know, I was on a verge of a new beginning, full of light and happiness.

After I failed the Bar, I moved to Russia. I spent the most memorable six months with my grandparents, met my fiancé, finished the first draft of my book, and began giving lectures in schools and universities about personal development.

Most of all, I stopped having any expectations of the future. I began trusting the divine intelligence to take me where I need to be. All I had to do is **set goals to create direction in life.** I had no idea any of this was going to happen! I was supposed to be enjoying my beautiful office at Littler Mandelson law firm as an associate.

The Universe has a plan of its own, and we will simply never know it. All we can do is do our best, and be honest with ourselves about that. We can hold ourselves accountable to do absolutely everything that is in our power to make our vision come true, everything. That means to work at our peak potential and stay as close to our deadlines as possible. But that's about it. If the Universe takes us somewhere else, then at least we can say we did what we could.

I used to get upset about breakups. Especially, when I would think that she was the one. I remember I used to scream to myself, "But she was perfect!" Then weeks, and sometimes months, after the breakup, I would realize that having her fully enter my life would have been the biggest mistake. Moreover, I would meet a new girl and think that she was the one.

Once I began to operate from the philosophy that the Universe is perfect, I stopped stressing about things working out according to my plan. There is a saying, "If you want to make God laugh, tell him about your plans." One of my clients asked me, "Dan, but how can I not stress about something that I really care for?"

His issue was that every time he would go to a job interview, he would get so worried, he would become emotionally wrecked by the time he even got to talk about the first thing on his resume. Obviously, he wouldn't get hired as a result. Sometimes, he wouldn't even go to an interview, because he would get too much into his head about how this will be just another failure that he is better off without.

He didn't trust the Universe, that was his problem. I told him, "Listen, if it is not meant for you to get this job, you will not get it, but there is absolutely no way for you to know that. The only thing you can do, is to do your best." Although this sounds like destiny talk, it isn't. It is more of a "put-your-100%-in" talk. This is why I stopped believing in destiny; we just don't know what the Universe has planned for us.

Same thing goes for relationships. If we are our best self in a relationship and we do everything reasonably necessary to make it work and it doesn't, forget it! Wasn't your person or wasn't your time. What can I say? There is only so much we can do.

What I found interesting, is that things that are meant to happen usually take very little effort on our part. All of the best jobs I've had I got almost without an interview. All the girls that turned out to be the best relationships, all found me. I did almost nothing to get them. They were just placed into my life at a perfect time, and they were very interested.

This will be an ongoing battle. Even if you completely adopt the philosophy that the Universe is perfect, there will still be moments in your life that will make you doubt that. When that happens, just try to give less of a fuck. Ultimately, this will help you save enormous amounts of energy.

The Universe is perfect, it makes no mistake.

Part II

MIND

Chapter 5

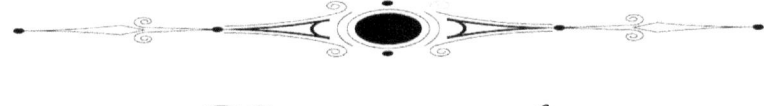

Reducing Stress

I remember I went on a vacation to Alicante in Spain. It is a beautiful city by the sea. It was my first time there, and I was amazed by the tranquil atmosphere of the city. Nobody was rushing and everyone was doing everything at their own pace. The fresh October air replenished my lungs with every breath. The warm sun rays felt so comforting. The vividly blue water filled the pupils of my eyes with color. The palm trees looked different than in Los Angeles; they seemed more tropical, which only added to the relaxing feeling of being on vacation.

I don't even know what day of the week it was, because that tends to happen when you are away from work. Whatever day it was, it turned out to be a turning point in my life. Sometimes, it takes just a moment, or one phrase you hear from a complete stranger at the right time. I was soon to discover that I was about to have a moment like that.

We were on this secluded beach when a man walked by and heard us speaking Russian, so he struck up a conversation with us. At first, we talked about the usual, where are we from, where is he from, what are we doing in Spain, and so on.

It turned out that he was the CFO of a company in Alicante. I immediately exclaimed, "Wow, handling all the finances must be tough." He shrugged and said, "It could be stressful, but not for me." I thought to myself, "I wish I could say that about my job," which at that time was a paralegal at a law office. My next thought was, "Wait a minute, how can being a CFO be less stressful than being a paralegal?"

I asked, "What do you mean by that?" At first, his face held a smile, but there was something about his smile. It wasn't the same as when someone is trying to soften what they are about to say. It was a smile of certainty, like he knew something the rest of the world didn't, and he knew the value of it. He said, "I don't think there is such thing as a stressful job, a stressful working environment, or stress in this world in general. Rather, there are people thinking stressful thoughts."

I disagreed with him immediately. I thought, "Of course there are stressful jobs! Take mine for example!" But I didn't say that. Instead, I asked, "Why do you think people think all these stressful thoughts?" His answer was simple and to the point, he said, "Because that's how they react."

I was so confused. Little did I know, that between those two phrases, the entire picture was complete. Two brush strokes are all it took. Everything that I had to know was right there, yet I had no idea what to do with it. It was only months later that I finally realized what all this meant.

That was probably the last vacation I went on where I laid on the beach and just relaxed. All of my vacations after that were excruciatingly intense. When I went to Italy, I woke up at six in the morning and explored the city for sixteen hours every day. Same thing with St. Petersburg, Iceland, and Japan. And this is how it is going to be with France when I go there again after this book is done.

I completely understand all those people who go on a vacation to take a break, I was certainly one of them. They think about how they will finally lie on the beach with some tropical drink in their hand and let the sun shine their worries away. They fantasize how they will turn their phones off, so that nobody would bother them. They dream of these five magical days a year when they will enjoy peace and take a break from stress. Then there are others who just never create stress in the first place, so there is nothing to take a break from.

Notice I said, "create." If we have the ability to create stress, then we have the ability to not create it. Many may think this means not creating the circumstances that lead to stress. However, that we can control. We can't get rid of our extenuating circumstances, our kids, traffic, or an obnoxious neighbor. Perhaps we could just move to the mountains. Oh, those Himalayan Mountains with no traffic and no obnoxious neighbors, how sweet would that be?

Interestingly enough, this is the mistake that many people make. They run away from stress, but it always finds them. They may switch jobs or move to a different neighborhood, and the first few months go smoothly. But then the old stressful circumstances find them at a new place or a new job. Different neighbor, different boss, different people, same obnoxious bastards.

Something always just miraculously happens, that causes them to experience stress all over again. Why is that? It is because they are the ones who create it. In creating it, they deprive themselves of the biggest solution to the problem, they deprive themselves of the choice not to be stressed, because we do indeed have it.

We Have a Choice

Many may disagree with this right away. Ironically, those are also usually the people who struggle with stress a lot. They live in this cause-and-effect world, where if an irritating and high-pressure event occurs, then they will be stressed, every time. They forget that it doesn't have to be this way. It is "that equals this" mentality. They have trained their body to react with stress over and over again, and now this reaction has been dug into their subconscious.

Moreover, their body may even have become addicted to this reaction. Here's an example, traffic. So many people let traffic irritate them to the point of insanity. You are stuck in traffic, again, just like the day before and the day before that, you get mad and curse the world. Did anything change? Are you less in traffic now?

It is such an emotional waste. Yet, many accept that if there is traffic, then they will be stressed, every time. On some days, there is no traffic, and so they feel good, but on the days when there is traffic, their lives are doomed.

What is happening, is that by reacting the same way to the same thing over time we condition the body to become addicted to that emotion, even if it is a negative one. We are firing and re-firing the same neurons repeatedly, and so the body begins to learn to react that way. Soon, that is all it knows. It is aware that if it reacts this way, it will receive the neurological stimulation it is used to. The body starts to crave its chemical fix.

Resultantly, we react the same way every time. That is when the feeling that we have a choice starts to slip away because we have to feed the addiction. So, the very first step toward reducing stress is to pull your mind out of the subconscious reaction, and bring it to conscious awareness. An awareness that you are doing what you just read. This can be done by asking yourself a simple question.

The next time an unfavorable event occurs and your body reacts the same way it always does, ask yourself, "Why is this irritating me? Why am I getting mad at traffic? Why am I getting pissed at my boss?"

You may not find a profoundly enlightening answer right away, but this will force your brain to catch itself in the moment of reacting subconsciously, and bring about that conscious awareness necessary to break the vicious cycle of stress. That is when you will start to see that you have a choice of how you *respond*.

Responding vs. Reacting

Our response is where we have the most control. That is where we have the most choice. **We may not be able to change our environment, but we can change how we respond to it.** The problem many people who are constantly stressed have is that they don't respond at all, they react.

They are like a thermometer that reacts to the temperature around them. The reason why this happens is because there is nothing in between the external stimuli and their reaction. Therefore, that reaction is loaded with emotions. To tackle this, we need to identify when stress happens.

Let's analyze two different attorneys in an identical situation, as an example. One reacts and the other one responds. Both work at a law office and both are having the most horrendously terrible day imaginable. Not only did they lose their keys in the morning, sacrificed a breakfast to a microwave explosion, found out that discovery responses are due today, and now they got a message that they blew a statute of limitations. At this point, they are feeling pretty ticked off.

The first attorney, who reacts, goes up in flames, punches a table, screams something out, and then immediately launches into a destructive army of thoughts such as, "I lost a bunch of money! I lost this case! The client will be pissed, and I will now be disciplined by the Bar!" These kinds of thoughts trigger what kind of emotions?

Very negative emotions, such as: anger, helplessness, despair, frustration, self-hate, and so on. Now here's the key moment, all of those emotions cause what? Stress. This just made his day very stressful, possibly even his entire week. That is a whole week of high cortisol levels, which all translates into a weakened immune system.

Let's back track, where did this start? Right when the external stimuli happened. Here, it was finding out that he blew a statute. He instantly found himself in an emotionally volatile state. This state is very dangerous, because that is when our feelings overshadow our rational mind. There's no cool-off period in which one can calm down, center their thoughts, and assess the situation logically.

Here, our first contender for a better life completely fucked it up, because after his unfortunate discovery, instead of pausing and taking a moment to cool off, he instantaneously lunged into tarnishing thoughts. Here's the big part, not one of those thoughts helped him solve the situation. *They only triggered emotions that then caused him enormous amounts of stress*, weakening his ability to solve anything.

Now, the second attorney, who responds, had an identical scenario happen to him. Initially, he also went up in flames, punched a table and screamed something out. He might have even felt horrible in the moment. But then, he paused. He took a step back, which gave him a second to cool off. In that pause, he created something very powerful. He created headspace — a space between the external stimuli and the response. It is in that space that he gave himself a choice to respond. Without that headspace, there is no choice to give oneself.

Calm and centered, he assessed the situation logically. He thought to himself, "This is awful, but how do I mitigate it?" He did not think of all of those destructive thoughts like the first attorney, instead, he sought a solution. *As a result, his thoughts never triggered emotions that caused him stress.*

Notice that it all starts with our perspective about the unfavorable event. Our perspective is made out of thoughts. For the first attorney, it was his emotionally charged, volatile thoughts that resulted in negative emotions and no solution to the problem. For the second attorney, it was his calm, collected thoughts that created the solution and helped him reduce stress.

External stimuli > REACTION >
volatile thoughts > negative emotions >**stress**

vs.

External stimuli — <u>headspace</u> — RESPONSE >
logical thoughts > no negative emotions > **less stress**

Where do our thoughts come from? From us! That is what the CFO in Alicante meant when he said, "There's no stress in this world, but rather people thinking stressful thoughts." Nobody is hijacking our brain and forcing us to think stressful thoughts. People do this to themselves.

The idea that your job, your boss, or people around you can make you stressed out originates from people who historically deprived themselves of a choice of how to respond to all of that. They also diminished their growth. An Austrian neurologist and psychiatrist, as well as the founder of logotherapy, Viktor Frankl said, "Between stimulus and response there is space. In that space lies our power to choose our response and, in that response, lies our growth and our freedom." The big question now is, how do we create that headspace?

The reason why some people will have a harder time with this than others is because for years, maybe even decades, they never created headspace. So, they have conditioned their body to always react, instead of respond. It is hard to rewire the circuitry of your brain overnight. Don't be surprised if it takes you anywhere from one to six months.

Here is what I do. When something happens, no matter how important, I try to care as little as possible. I just stare blankly into space and pretend that I am in the most unbreakable Zen mode imaginable. In that moment, I try to blank my mind by not thinking about what just happened, or what I have to do. I take a step back, and look at the situation from the third-person perspective, as if this did not just happen to me but to someone else. This allows me to take a break and retract from the occurrence for about four to five seconds. That is enough to create headspace.

However, every day the world tries to test us, and so we have to remain strong. When we create headspace, in a way, we say, "Fuck you" to that what tries to test us, that it is not going to tell us how to feel, what to feel, and when to feel it, because WE decide that, nothing and no one else does. Remember that and take control of your life.

Healthy Stress

A small dosage of stress actually is healthy because, among many things, it increases focus and attention. It is also necessary in certain situations, when we have to activate the fight or flight response. This is especially important when we find ourselves in dangerous or threatening situations. So, there are times when stress is appropriate, but always living in this state depletes our energy and leaves us with nothing to create.

Don't Let the Venom Spread

Time may heal all the wounds, but understand that we choose how deep those wounds are. One of the top most dangerous professions is milking venomous snakes. The venom is sold to hospitals and pharmaceutical companies. I thought, who would ever do a job like that? But fifty thousand dollars for a small vial, answered that question.

What is inevitable in this business is getting bit by a snake. However, it is interesting that not a single person has ever died from a snakebite itself. Instead, people died from the venom that spread through their bloodstreams. We do not die from the tragic event itself; we die from the effect we allow it to have on us. That is why the same tragedy can kill some and not even touch others. Notice that initially, the second lawyer had the same response as the first, because it is natural. However, the second lawyer did not let the venom spread into his bloodstream.

If you make something a big deal, it becomes a big deal. Why? Because the more attention you give something, the more you feed it with energy. Our focus is very powerful. This is perfectly measurable. You spend five minutes focusing on a problem, it is a five-minute problem. You spend a day focusing on a problem, it becomes a day-long problem. So, we have to learn to minimize the importance of things. For that, we have to re-evaluate what is important to us in the first place.

What is most important to you? Many may say family, money, or success. Nevertheless, without health, all of those are meaningless. We cannot enjoy our money if we cannot get out of bed; we cannot be a part of our children's lives if we do not have the health to attend their basketball games; we cannot feel successful if we are sick. Meanwhile, stress is absolutely the main cause of most health problems:

Unhealthy Stress

Specifically, it is the prolonged stress that causes the reduction of the salivary immunoglobulin A — a chemical that is one of the main proteins responsible for a healthy immune system. The reduction of this protein leads to a weakened immune response. One of the main things that lowers salivary immunoglobulin A is cortisol, which is a stress hormone. [2] For that reason, aside from tarnishing our spirituality and our lives as spiritual beings, stress also leads to the following health conditions:

---

[2] Dispenza, Becoming Supernatural, p. 78.

Heart attack

The body responds to physical, mental, or emotional pressure by releasing stress hormones such as *epinephrine* and *norepinephrine* that increase blood pressure, increased heart rate, and raise blood sugar levels. Frequent releases of these hormones over time can put an extra strain on your heart, damaging it, and blood supply to other areas of your body fails. Over time this may lead to chest pains and eventually a heart attack.[3]

Kidney damage

An adequate supply of blood is needed to keep kidneys working properly. When a clot or heart damage reduces your kidneys' blood supply, they have to work harder to filter poisons and get rid of excess wastes. Your kidneys scar and shrink. They cannot work properly, and you can die from poisoning or kidney failure. [4]

Stress headaches

Stress can trigger a migraine headache. In times of emotional stress, certain chemicals are released that provoke the vascular changes that cause that to happen. After a stressful period, there may be a letdown which can, in itself, trigger a migraine headache. A migraine's pain is enough to numb a person's limbs, blur vision, and make them feel nauseated. [5]

Stroke

Stress raises your blood pressure and cholesterol levels. This can cause a blood clot to form. The clot travels to the brain, becomes lodged, blocks the blood flow to the brain, and cause a stroke. High blood pressure can also cause a blood vessel in the brain to burst. Strokes can cause paralysis, brain damage, and death. [6]

---

[3] Bhatt, "'Stress' cardiomyopathy: A different kind of heart attack," Harvard Health Blog, September 03, 2015
[4] National Kidney Foundation, "You and your kidneys", June 6, 2020
[5] National Headache Foundation, "Stress," News blog, Oct. 25, 2007
[6] Flint Rehab and Maher, "Can Stress Cause a Stroke: What You Need to Know", Neurological Recovery Blog, August 26, 2020

Arteriosclerosis

The argument is made that people reacting to stressors, which are not life-threatening but are "perceived" as such, mount similar stress/inflammatory responses in the arteries, and which, if repetitive or chronic, may culminate in atherosclerosis. When you are under stressful conditions, your blood cholesterol rises. The cholesterol can build up in your arteries and slow your blood flow. Your heart must pump harder. Your blood pressure rises. Your arteries harden and take a rough, irregular shape. A clot can form and block blood flow entirely, causing death. [7]

Skin disorder

Stress also promotes the release of hormones into your system. Some abnormalities may result on your skin because your body chemistry changes. You may develop a rash, acne, or other inflammation. Your lowered resistance to disease also allows fungal infections like athlete's foot. [8]

Tumor

Stress induces signals that cause cells to develop into tumors, Yale researchers have discovered. Because stress weakens the body's immune system, abnormal cells easily invade healthy tissue. The cells divide rapidly, and too much tissue is produced. If the tumor is cancerous, it can be deadly. Cancer can spread to other areas through the bloodstream or lymphatic system. [9]

So, next time something happens that normally triggers you, ask yourself, "Is this really worth my health?" When somebody cuts you off in traffic, and you blow up in flames ready to get back at them, ask yourself, "Is this important enough to waste my health on?" When your significant other says something that just makes you wonder why did you ever marry this person, you could feel your heart rate immediately shooting up, and you may even feel pain in your stomach, ask yourself, "Is this worth it?"

---

[7] Black, and Garbutt, "Stress, inflammation and cardiovascular disease", National Library of Medicine, January 2002.
[8] Munn, "Does stress cause skin problems?" All Healthy Me articles, January 20, 2017.
[9] Yale News, "Stress Triggers Tumor Formation, Yale Researchers Find", January 13, 2010

If you run this question by everything in your life that causes you stress, you will quickly see that nothing is more important than your health, so anything or anyone causing you stress, by default, is not important. Therefore, one thing we must never forget is that we have a choice of how we respond to the world around us. We must not deprive ourselves of that choice, because that is where the path to peace, happiness, and spiritual magnetism truly lies, in our unaffectedness.

Choose to respond with calmness.

.

Chapter 6

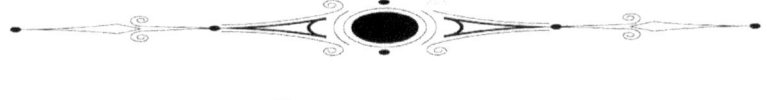

Meditation

You might have noticed that a large portion of the previous chapter about stress had to do with controlling your thoughts. In order to take a pause and create that headspace, we have to be able to tell ourselves to stop thinking for a moment. That is the only thing that allows us to retract from the situation.

There are two reasons why some people may struggle with this at first. First, they may not be able to have the mind control necessary to tell themselves to take a break, even for four to five seconds. Second, they may not have the level of awareness required to recognize that they are about to slip down the familiar path of an immediate reaction. This happens all of the time; we may react to something in a volatile manner, and then after it's over, we think back and say, "I didn't even realize I did that." Meditation helps us overcome those two limitations and open our eyes to a new level of awareness and control.

To me, meditation is just that, awareness. An awareness of everything: thoughts, feelings, surroundings, people, and even our internal flow of energy. Meditation is the essence of being present, and being present is the essence of enjoying your life. For many people, meditation has this negative stigma, because they think it is some far-fetched spiritual nonsense. It can be spiritual, but I know plenty of people who don't consider themselves spiritual or religious who meditate regularly. In reality, it is very practical.

To understand how it can help us deal with stress, and eventually other negative emotions such as anger, doubt, regret, and many others, we have to understand how it works.

You see, our mind is naturally active. We are always thinking about something, even when we are unaware of it. Some statistics claim that on average, we experience 65,000 thoughts a day! Meditation helps us clear our mind of all of those thoughts. But what does this really mean? As you recall, our thoughts trigger emotions, so if we can clear our thoughts, then we can get rid of the emotions that they are causing us. Here is how…

There are many different types of meditations. I personally practice six different ones, depending on what I want to achieve. The one I started out with, was the emptying my mind meditation. It has nothing to do with breathing. It focuses on one thing and one thing only, to stare into the darkness behind your eyelids and think about nothing.

You have to sit in a comfortable position, close your eyes with your palms facing up. The key is to not move, because as still as your body is, is as still as your mind should be. When you close your eyes, try to look into the dark space in front of you. After a few seconds, you may have a thought bombard your focus. It's okay, just become aware that you are experiencing a thought, and shift it to the side, regaining your concentration on the darkness. In a single meditation session, in the beginning, it is okay to repeat this process over sixty times. So, don't feel discouraged if it feels like it's not working at first.

Notice what is happening: awareness and control. Just as how, during meditation, we first become aware of the thought that tries to break our focus and then shift it to the side, in a stressful situation, we can first become aware of the reactive thought that we experience and then shift it to the side, creating headspace. Only then, can we formulate a response. The ability to pause lies in our ability to tell ourselves, "STOP." What do we do during mediation? Same thing.

When I started, I could not stay focused for more than three seconds. I would focus on the dark space, and become almost immediately distracted. There was a time when I gave up on meditation altogether because of this very reason. But then, I had a realization.

First, I understood that meditation is not about emptying your mind, but rather the process of becoming aware of your thoughts and shifting them to the side. The repetition of this exercise is what strengthens our control over our mind! The more we tell ourselves, "Focus on this and not on that," the more our mind listens to us. The more control we have over our cognitive processes, the less we can be affected by the hardships of the human experience.

Second, I realized that this is what the word "mindfulness" meant! It is the ultimate awareness. If one is aware of their thoughts, one is aware of their emotions. Why? Think back on a time when you came back from work and you had this uneasy feeling, but you couldn't really understand where it was coming from. At dinner, you were quiet. You tried to watch your favorite show after, but couldn't really enjoy it. When you finally made it to bed, you told your significant other that you had a rough day and shut the lights off.

Only the next morning while driving to work, after not feeling a great deal of relief, you finally asked yourself, "Where is this feeling coming from?" Now let's throw an imaginary character, John, into your shoes.

John thought about it, and after some reflection, he remembered a moment when his boss said something embarrassing about him in front of the team, but everyone just laughed it off, and so it didn't seem like a big deal. Yet that comment was true, so John thought, "Man, now they all know." That caused him to feel not only embarrassment, but also some guilt. He rationalized, "My boss' intentions weren't bad, overall, he values me." He realized what he felt and the cause of it. That allowed him to then deal with those emotions. As a result, he immediately felt better.

Do you see what just happened? Only when John traced his uneasy feeling back to a particular thought that caused it, and became aware of the emotions it triggered, was he able to resolve them. This is mindfulness.

Imagine if he never asked himself, "Where is this feeling coming from?" That is exactly how many of us end up with unresolved emotions that become so suppressed we cannot even trace them back anymore. They just rot inside of us, affecting our mood, then our temper, and eventually our character. Without mindfulness, it is so much harder to become aware of the thoughts that drive our feelings.

Remember I said how meditation can also help us manage anger and other negative emotions? It is the same model. When we experience a thought and we **believe** it, it creates an emotion. An emotion is a chemical that gets dumped into our bloodstream, which is what makes us feel what we feel.

If a friend you trust came up to you and told you that your car burned down, you would experience a thought of your car burning down. Then, you would believe it, and that is when you would experience emotions such as worry, fear, and distress. The chemicals of those three emotions get sent into your bloodstream, and you could feel your heart rate increasing, palms getting sweaty, anxiety, shortness of breath, and over all this heavy, negative feeling would cast its dark shadow upon you.

However, if you got a random call that showed up as spam on your caller ID, and the person on the line told you that your social security number has been compromised, you would experience a thought that would process what you just heard, but you wouldn't believe it, and so there would be no negative emotion ever created.

It is what we believe that creates the emotions. We can't stop thinking; thoughts will always enter our mind naturally. What we can control, however, is our focus and our belief. Yet, it all starts with mindfulness.

After a thought enters your mind, you can either believe it or not. You can either focus on it or place your attention elsewhere. You can believe in a reality that doesn't stress you out, or you can believe in a reality that makes you lose your shit. You can give your focus to something that aggravates you, or to something that brings you peace.

If you start believing in something that makes you feel uneasy, ask yourself, "Is this a fact? Can I independently verify this?" If you cannot independently verify it, it's not a fact, and as much as you may think it is true, just be ready for it to be false. Think of how much energy this simple analysis could save us.

I will never forget a woman I met, who thought that her husband was cheating on her. She never caught him cheating or had any facts to show, but she just *knew*. She knew she could trust her womanly instinct, and it told her just that. She could not get this belief out of her head. It haunted her in every move her husband made.

Every time he would come home late from work, pick up a call at night, cancel a dinner date, she would believe that it was because of another woman. He tried to talk to her, but she was set in her beliefs. The husband began to resent her because she was acting this way, and he started to avoid her as much as possible. This made her even more suspicious, and after many months of aggravation and stress, she decided to pull the trigger.

The divorce really affected their two daughters. They didn't take it well, nor did she. She put herself through psychological trauma, thousands of dollars to attorneys, split all of the community property, and lost her trust in men.

After a few years, she learned the truth. Her husband had a drug addiction that he did not dare to tell anyone, not even her, in fear that it would affect his reputation as a public figure and as a father. His wife's behavior made him want to remove himself even more into the sweet and comforting injected dopamine rushes that took him to a different place, away from all the marital problems. Turned out, he was loyal to her the whole time. Ugh... if only she was more mindful.

So, no matter how absolutely sure, without a single doubt, you may think you are, unless it is a fact, just know that you could be utterly wrong. **Unless you can independently verify it, it's a belief — and beliefs may be true or false.** Our inner dialogue is full of unsubstantiated beliefs. Meditation helps us silence that dialogue, but it may not always help.

If the thought is so troubling that no meditation can silence it, talk to your inner voice. Ask, "Can there be another possibility? How do I know for sure?" That woman could have saved her marriage and her two girls, if she would have asked herself those two simple questions.

There are facts and there are beliefs. A blue couch is a blue couch. It is not purple, or yellow, or black; if it is blue, it is blue. That is a fact. On the other hand, "A girl stood me up because she does not like me," is a belief. It feels so true, and your mind will make up stories validating your beliefs, because we want to be right. It feels good to be right. Yet, the girl could have not shown up because her car exploded, or she had an emergency.

You know what you know, you don't know what you don't know. Next time you experience an inner battle of thoughts and beliefs, just remember, **you are not always right.**

In addition to reducing stress and negative emotions, there is another sacred benefit to meditation. Our mind is always racing. It fills us with thoughts of what is happening, what we think is happening, and what we think will happen. Our mind is like a mountain river with the water running so fast, we cannot see the bottom. Yet on the bottom of the river, there may be infinite worlds of information that could be used to live an extraordinary life.

If we put a flood gate at the end of the river, and a flood gate at the beginning of it, the water will slow down and eventually stop. Only then, will one see the bottom with little rocks, fishes, and intricate sand patterns. Our mind is the same way. Except that on the bottom, we will see our true self.

A constant flow of thoughts takes us out of the present, and separates us from who we truly are. In our constant mental chatter, we lose contact with our inner self. Meditation helps us slow it down.

I remember I was about twenty-four and had been meditating close to two months. I closed my eyes and concentrated on the darkness. As usual, thoughts began to interrupt my efforts. In the dark, I saw many little moving particles. I felt like I couldn't center myself. Then suddenly, the particles began to clear up, as if I began moving through them and passed them toward something, but I didn't know what. I felt like I was dissolving into relaxation, and everything was beginning to slow down.

Then, in an instant, the particles cleared up, and here it was, stationary, clear, uninterrupted darkness. I felt like I was on the other side. I almost felt detoxed. Yet most of all, I felt like I was looking into the sanctified window of my subconscious. For the first time, I was one on one with myself.

At that time in my life, I was confused as to why although everything was going well (I had a good job, nice car, beautiful girlfriend, a place in sunny California), I just couldn't stop drinking.

I just couldn't understand why I had to drink until I blacked out every single time. What was I trying to suppress? It just was never enough. I had to drink more and more, as if I was chasing the dragon that I could never catch. I didn't understand what it was about the impulse. Was it the high, was it the hype, was it the energy?

Here is the crazy part: when I would feel completely fucked up with no more space to drink, I would drink more. How much I bought is how much I had to drink, no matter what. I could not keep alcohol in the house. I would just do anything possible to empty it. No matter how I felt. Nothing mattered.

It was amazing and horribly terrifying. No matter how much I reasoned, how much I thought about it, how much I said no … the alcohol was stronger. I had no idea why I was so weak. It turned out that it wasn't me who was weak, it was the connection to my subconscious that was weak, and in my subconscious is where the reason to my struggle lay.

During this meditation, all of the noise dissipated. So did all of the thoughts that kept me away from looking into myself for all those years! It was like everyone left the room after a big party, and I was standing in the middle of the floor by myself, just me, for the first time. I finally realized why I was drinking.

I remembered that when I was seventeen, I wasn't popular, and the only friends I had were in school. I was trying to gain acceptance among the Russian community in Northeast Philadelphia. All of the kids there had cars, girls, were going out and living an adult life. I began drinking with them.

It wasn't about the feeling of being drunk, it was the feeling of fitting in. It was never about the alcohol at that time. I never even had thoughts of getting a bottle to get drunk, or let alone drink by myself. Acceptance into their circle, into that lifestyle, that's what it was about. It felt amazing and I loved it.

The only thing is that even after I was fully integrated into that social circle, I continued drinking. As time passed by, the day I started drinking slowly dissolved into the past. With that, the memory of why I started sank deeper to the river's floor of my subconscious, until I became completely unaware of it altogether.

It was during that meditation session that I was able to bring up what was lost. I realized that I drank because I associated drinking with that transformative part of my life, where I began to be accepted and it felt incredible. The feeling of being drunk and the feeling of belonging were one. Acceptance was such a highly charged emotion, that it continued to manipulate me through my subconscious into my drinking habits.

Our subconscious is our body's operating system. Many things we do, we may not even realize why we do them. But there is a reason to every single action we take. Because I was so caught up in the moment and in my thoughts, I couldn't see down to the bottom of the river.

To see the truth about ourselves, we have to stop the mental chatter, and only then can we observe the submerged truth behind our problems, our feelings, and ourselves. Silencing the mind allows us to learn a lot about ourselves because it is precisely our mind that restricts us from looking into the subconscious reasons behind our actions, habits, thoughts, and patterns. Until we silence our mind, we can't live an extraordinary life.

Therefore, meditation is not only practical when it comes to reducing stress and negative emotions, it is the ultimate path to self-realization. After that day, I stopped drinking.

Chapter 7

Anger

Wholistic living lies in living balanced. This is why this book is about the ultimate spirit, mind, body mastery. When we are balanced, we excel with ease much faster in many areas of our life. I have met people who were very spiritual, and took care of their body, but had no ambition for financial growth. I have met very ambitious individuals, who did not care about their body, and so their health problems slowed them down tremendously. I also have met people who were in fantastic shape and very smart, but their inability to deal with their emotions — mainly anger — destroyed their professional and personal relationships.

Everything is interconnected. If we lack balance in one part of our life it will always affect another. What throws us out of balance the most, in my opinion, is anger. When we are angry, a number of things can begin to spiral down: our health, our relationships, our ability to solve problems, and not to mention, don't hope for a spiritual enlightenment of self-realization when you are ticked off.

What is ironic is that anger is actually our most primal way of restoring balance. It is our body's attempt to "quick fix" the injustice. There are, however, a multitude of problems related to this immediate, push-back reaction. The key one is that it almost never resolves the issue that made us angry. If anything, it usually makes it worse.

We may feel angry when we feel threatened or attacked, frustrated or powerless, invalidated, or treated unfairly, or not respected. Yet, please realize that there is not a single person or event in this world that can ever *make* you angry. It is your reaction to them that jacks up your heart rate. We will talk more about that later.

For now, here is what is fascinating: nobody is born angry. Perhaps, just a little bit, because stepping into this world is such a poor trade-off compared to how sweet we have it in the mother's womb. But I did back in 1991, and we all did it.

During the course of my career as a life mentor, I came across some very angry people. I tried to envision them as babies when they were just born, and I thought to myself, "What happened?" Here is what happened.

Just like with stress, if we constantly react with anger, over time, our body becomes conditioned to this reaction. Emotions are chemicals that get released into our bloodstream. **Our brain monitors our chemical state, and the moment we feel angry, it will think more corresponding thoughts equal to how we feel.** As a result, more chemicals of anger get released into our bloodstream, which begin to signal our hormone centers. [10]

The hormonal centers that get signaled are the adrenal glands. As the adrenal glands release their hormones, we begin feeling pretty mad. This stores the energy of anger into the mind of our body — the subconscious. Remember how in Chapter Three I said, "What you put out is what you put in"? If you put in anger, you put out anger. This is how this actually happens.

All of that emotion that was originally created from your thoughts, becomes stored as energy of anger in the body. That's why when we get squeezed, more anger comes out. You might have noticed, when you meet people with anger problems, you can sometimes feel that energy, which can be a very uncomfortable feeling.

Notice that once again it all starts with your thoughts, which trigger your belief, which creates emotion, which turns into this chemical dump. If you think a thought that your apartment's manager is unfair, that turns on a neurological network in your brain. That makes you think another corresponding thought to that emotion, perhaps, that she pisses you off, and that turns on another neurological network in your brain. Then that

---

[10] Bailey, (director). *E-Motion 2.0*, 2014.

makes you think yet another corresponding thought to that emotion, and you think that you are paying too much to be treated this way — and now you are pretty ticked off.

If you think enough thoughts on the same vibrational frequency, and activate enough of the same neurological networks in a specific pattern, you produce a certain internal representation of yourself.

Your belief remains the controlling factor. Imagine if you chose to believe that the manager gets a lot of pressure from the corporate owner, and gets threatened to lose her job if she doesn't follow the protocol, so, in reality, she has nothing against you. Would you feel differently?

Yet when you go down the rabbit hole of angry, negative thoughts, you would never even consider believing that alternative. Which is understandable; these are not corresponding thoughts. Thoughts attract other thoughts of their kind, negativity attracts negativity, anger attracts anger.

Why? This has nothing to do with the law of attraction. It is because when you react with anger, the message that you are sending to your brain is, "Send me another reason to feel the way I'm already feeling, send me another reason to feel angry." The redundancy of this process can go on for decades, and that is how beautifully born babies become angry people. Just as a side note: in the same exact way, people become pessimistic, victims, negative, emotionally vulnerable, and so on. Same pattern, different emotions, same outcome.

In the example above, you see yourself as an angry person. If you accept, believe, and surrender to that identity, then you become that way on a subconscious level. Over time, you store more and more energy that results from corresponding thoughts of an angry, frustrated, negative person. Those emotions become so familiar to you that you begin to think that's who you are. At that point, your magnetism is polluted with this kind of energy, and so you attract more events, people, and circumstances that make you angry.

Think about this: **your internal identity is a memorized set of automatic thoughts, reflective emotional reactions, unconscious habits, behaviors, and routine familiar attitudes.** The body becomes programmed to react to certain situations — and all similar situations — in the same way, every time, causing you to experience more emotions that you are better off without.

"The more you recreate the same loop of thinking and feeling and feeling and thinking you will continue to store the energy in the energy centers of your body. This begins to produce a biological effect."[11] In this case, it can be adrenal fatigue, digestive problems, kidney issues, or a weakened immune system. Also, other psychological effects, such as shortened temper, impatience, frustration, or intolerance, will arise. You continue to hardwire your brain in this pattern, and you continue to condition the body to become this way.[12]

To break the pattern, we first have to pull the mind out of the subconscious. If it stays there, we have no access to the root of our reactions to our human experience. This is why a lot of people never change, but only continue becoming more angry, more pessimistic, and more swallowed into the dark patterns of their thinking and feeling loop.

How do we pull the mind out of the subconscious? We look at the other side of things. In the beginning of this book, I told you the only thing you really have to change is your perspective.

Consider driving your car and having some guy cut you off. You can believe that he doesn't care about anybody, and he cut you off on purpose. How will you feel? However, that guy could have a dying mother in the hospital, and he is rushing to say his last words to her. Does that change how you feel about him?

How do you know which reality is true? You don't. There is no way for you to know, one way or another. You will never really know a lot of things, and frankly, it doesn't matter. What matters is which truth makes you feel more at peace? Remember, **you always have a choice what to**

<hr />

[11] Dispenza, Becoming Supernatural: How Common People Are Doing the Uncommon. Audiobook, Chapter 5
[12] Dispenza, Becoming Supernatural: How Common People Are Doing the Uncommon. Audiobook, Chapter 5.

believe. So, believe that what makes you feel better, until you, someone, or something disproves it. Even then, you still have a choice.

There are many arguments that the virus that caused the pandemic of 2020 was man-made, specifically to reduce the planet's population. Believing that would make me angry. So, I chose not to. Regardless of how many arguments I heard in support of that. Because, why? Am I going to change the situation in any way, by believing one reality over another? Will fewer people die? Will more schools re-open? The only thing that will change is my mood and the amount of energy I waste. I can't tell you enough how many people lost their minds over this pandemic for nothing.

There is always another side, and we have to always explore it to break the patterns of what we conditioned our body to do. And if that doesn't work, then welcome to Chapter Eight.

Chapter 8

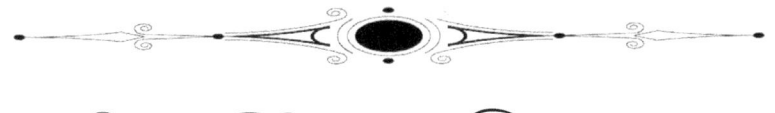

The Power of Calmness

In my opinion, calmness is the ultimate life mastery. Why? A lot comes with it. When we possess the inner discipline of calmness, we have much more control. The more control we have, the less others can control us. In the moment when someone ticks you off, you are a puppet in their hands. They can do whatever they want with you. They can make you do irrational things, lose your train of thought, make poor decisions, and then regret all of it later. Calmness is like a veil that makes us untouchable. The stronger our discipline, the stronger our calmness, the thicker the veil. That is why, in a sense, to me, calmness is freedom.

I think, calmness is also peace. When we are calm, we slow down our emotions of worry, anxiety, endless desire, and anger, which all diminish a peaceful state of being. As a result, when we are at peace, we are very empathetic and passionate because we have the emotional availability to be so. Our emotions are not wasted on all the negativity that makes us insensitive and hateful. The greater the calmness, the greater the peace, the greater the ability to live a more joyful, happy life.

Beyond that, mastering the inner discipline of calmness helped me in my career.

As an attorney, I faced many difficult situations. However, none of them compared to the hardships my boss put opposing counsels and their clients through. For the longest time, I couldn't figure out whether this was all strategic, or if my boss was just evil.

Depositions were his mastery, because that is when he would really get under the skin of the defense and the deponent. He would say the most outrageous shit imaginable. He never violated any rules of professional responsibility, he knew them very well, but he would get as close to that borderline as possible. It wrecked the opposing side to the point that they couldn't even function anymore. They would lose all common sense.

My boss would get them so aggravated they would start acting irrationally, forgetting facts, making mistakes. Some lawyers even breached their duties to the client. It was like my boss had a way of tapping into their operating system and disconnecting all the wires so they would start malfunctioning. It was amazing how top-level professionals easily allowed their emotions to get the best of them, even when thousands of dollars and their client's future were at stake. Except for Steve.

White guy, bold, grey suit, white shirt with thin black stripes, dark green tie, no watch, nice black leather shoes, but nothing fancy. He was very polite and courteous, but straight to the point. He was a type of person who didn't waste your time, and didn't want you to waste his. He was a no-bullshit type of guy, and he made sure you knew that.

I've seen people like that before, and my boss just wrecked them without forgiveness. We go into the deposition. I remember I was so excited because the opposing side really screwed up in this case. I got my front row seats and popcorn ready. About an hour in, the show begins. My boss gets into his regular I'm-about-to-roast-you tone of voice, and I'm thinking, "Here we go."

My boss starts bringing up how the other side was evasive, followed up by concealment of evidence. Then he goes into, "What do you think will happen?" type of speech. He tells them what it will be and how he will make sure of it. If I was on the other side of that table at this point and someone would have said something like this to my client, if they didn't start crying, I would for them. The way he said it was just so piercing.

I expected Steve to go up in flames and start apprehensively screaming out objections. Steve remained absolutely stationary. He was completely unaffected by any of this. He knew it was true and he knew his client was in deep shit, but he did not show a single sign. He calmly asked my boss to specify exactly the documents that he was referring to, and moved on from there.

I was taken back, and my boss was thrown off. He looked at me like, "This usually does it." He proceeded with more disabling questions, cleverly crafted to bury the opposing side. Yet no matter how much we called them out on the facts that significantly undermined his case, Steve remained unmoved.

I couldn't even tell how he felt inside, because on the surface he was cool, calm, collected, and most of all, convincing. It's like he was untouchable. Nothing that my boss said even for a second disturbed his train of thought and his perfectly phrased robust objections.

Steve figured out a clear route to take his client out of a losing case, and executed it. He made sure nobody was going to sway him away from his objective. Just relentless, laser beam focus on the prize, no matter what. Steve made his arguments, he protected his client and he left, without having his heart rate increase even a beat. I was fascinated.

Calmness is power, calmness is freedom. We all have the ability to strengthen it. If people are not born angry but become angry, what does this mean? We somehow manage to change ourselves to be a certain way. Unfortunately, most of the time a negative change happens on its own, while a positive one we have to consciously facilitate.

I'm sure we can all relate. We may change when life hits us with betrayal, a great loss, abandonment, or violence (just to name a few), over and over again. We may start to look at things differently, become bitter, pessimistic, or angry. This is because our brain is ever evolving. In a way, this is good news, because no matter how stuck in your ways you may feel, if you got there somehow, it is just as possible that you can get out of there.

Yes, it is harder to undo the damage to the house rather than build it right from the start, especially when you are ongoingly chipping away its pieces. The way we condition ourselves to react angrily to certain situations or people is the same way we can condition ourselves to respond with calmness. For that, we will need everything we talked about up to this point.

As discussed in the previous chapter, to create a change, we have to pull the mind out of the subconscious. Otherwise, we will continue doing what we have been doing automatically all along. For this, we need a certain level of mindfulness. If our reactions to the external stimuli continue going unnoticed, then we cannot fix it.

When you take your car to a repair shop, the mechanic first has to become aware of what the problem is in order to fix it. Same thing with us; we cannot begin to recondition our body to respond with calmness, if we don't even notice ourselves responding with anger. As discussed in Chapter Six, in my opinion, meditation is the fastest way to increase one's mindfulness. It helps tremendously.

Be prepared that this will be a gradual process. Your mind and your body like their routine, and you will be pulling them out of it. Naturally, they will resist. They will send you all of these cleverly designed thoughts, like, "It's not working, this is all nonsense, it's too late to change," and so on. Listen, acknowledge, discredit. Know that you can never go wrong by responding with calmness. Treat it like learning a new skill.

For example, learning to write with your other hand feels hard. You are so used to picking up the pen with your writing hand, your fingers automatically know how to hold it, and you write instinctively without even thinking. It is easy for you. Changing hands will feel monumental.

At first, it will feel wrong to even pick up the pen with the other hand, let alone write with it. It would feel difficult, uncomfortable, and unnatural. The same way it will feel when you start trying to respond with calmness to aggravating people or events. Don't get discouraged. When you were a kid learning to write for the first time, it also felt the same way. Yet you conditioned yourself to master that skill.

After about thirty attempts, it will start to feel easier to respond with calmness to everything, not just stressful and aggravating situations, but pressuring, unwelcoming, demanding events as well. The key is to not skip an opportunity. **Every single aggravating, stressful, and difficult occurrence, person, or event that is sent your way by the Universe is your**

opportunity to practice responding with calmness. Don't get angry and miss one; that would be a waste. The Universe is perfect; it may not always send you what you want, but it sure sends you what you need.

Our human experience can be unforgiving. All of the health problems that you read about in the chapter about reducing stress occur because of people's unwillingness to respond differently. How many people do you know who are unhappy because they are always pissed off about something? It's like something always gives them the reason to feel that way, something always happens. Once they overcome one problem, the next one is on the rise, ready to ruin their day and sometimes their life.

Many people break under this kind of pressure. They start making excuses that when they get home they have to drink or get high because they had a stressful day. Then the excuses turn into addictions, and eventually, very unhappy lives. It is a downward spiral.

This is why we must learn to remain calm and unaffected. Just like Steve. During meditation when we sit still, that is how still our mind must be even during volatile situations. A concrete beam that is dug into the ground only a foot can be easily swayed; a concrete beam that extends twenty feet under the ground is inflexible. We have to learn to be inflexible.

Calmness helps us conserve our energy, and use it when we need it most. People with volatile personalities do not have this ability, because they run their energy thin. This is why in martial arts they teach students to stay calm, so then when the time comes, they can strike with all of their energy that they have conserved.

As you remember, we talked about the ultimate goal in life, and we concluded that our whole life is a persistent battle for energy. So why waste that which we work so hard for?

This should not be confused with suppressing emotions. If a stressful situation arises and you react with anger, and then you try to be calm instead of feeling it and dealing with that emotion, that is suppressing the anger. This should be avoided. Once you react with anger, for example, the damage has been done. You already fell into the puddle with mud and now you are trying to clean yourself off. Moreover, now you have placed the energy of anger into your magnetism and are more likely to attract more events that will make you angry. Responding with calmness is walking around the puddle and never getting dirty in the first place.

Calmness brings us happiness; calmness brings us peace. Calmness is freedom, power, and strength.

Chapter 9

Let's Not Regret

To truly cleanse our magnetism and become more aligned with the Universe's guidance, we must let go of everything that clutters our spiritual energy. We already talked about how negative thoughts, stress, and anger, can tightly wrap the heavy chains around our ankles, preventing us from taking a leap into the life we want to live. Another very common negative emotion that weighs us down and weakens our magnetism is regret.

An important question that we can all easily relate to is how do you feel when you experience regret? Happy, alive, friendly, outgoing? No, we feel down, we feel unexcited, tired or depressed, certainty not happy. That is because just like many other negative emotions, it takes away our energy that we fight so hard for.

Let's take it a step further. What happens when we experience regret? We are thinking about something unfavorable that happened or that we did. As you remember "Where our attention goes, our energy flows." This means that we are now feeding the feeling of regret with our attention, expanding its negative magnetic charge inside of us, and therefore aligning ourselves with the vibrations of another situation we could regret later. Since we are magnetic beings with the ability to attract, what do you think we will be attracting, if our attention is on that which we regret?

There are different kinds of regret. Many people regret what they have or have not done. They say things would be different right now, only if…. Maybe you're right, maybe you're wrong. I remember I used to regret doing this one trick that resulted in me tearing the ligaments in my knee. However, that injury allowed me to ascend as an athlete.

I started training differently, stretching, conditioning and developed a mind-body connection I could have never dreamed of.

Therefore, all the times you told yourself, "I just wish I did that," is a complete waste of energy. Something that may feel like a mistake right now, may turn out to be the biggest blessing tomorrow. You just don't know; only the Universe or God or Allah or the field of energy around us knows.

For me, it was a combination of two things that created an internal shift of perspective. First, I got so tired of telling myself what I wished I didn't or did do. I felt helpless every time, because the opportunity was gone. Second, I was so tired of being proven wrong. So many things that I believed were punishments, turned out to be gifts from the Universe. Take the shortcut and remember, **there is absolutely nothing that you should have done. The Universe is perfect.**

Regret keeps us stuck in the past. Yes, learn from your mistakes, but then move on. **The trail you leave behind, will never move you forward.** The more we hold on to the emotional pain of regret, the greater the pain gets. The faster you let go of it, the faster the wounds heal. This is why regret inhibits progress.

I can't tell you enough how many people I've met who don't let themselves heal, because they can't let go. The minute they finally begin to move on just a little toward the warm sunny rays of the new future, they remind themselves of what they did wrong, and the cold, sharp, piercing sorrow punctures the flesh of their soul and they bleed again. This is crucial, because until we let go, we cannot move forward in anything. A part of us will be consumed by that act we wish we had or hadn't done. While the feeling of never getting another chance or not being able to rehabilitate the situation only makes it worse. This is why once we finally accept the past, we will always feel relief. Be mindful of this.

Many of my potential clients were older than me, and they asked, "How are you supposed to mentor me if I have more years under the belt?" I love that question because it is the first indicator that they should be my client. You can live forty years mindless and learn nothing, or four years mindful and learn enough to teach others.

There is no point in regretting what we did. We already did it. However, you have all the reason to regret not trying to make it right, or to do the things you always wanted. And to avoid that, we have to not fear to try.

Chapter 10

Fear is Growth

Fear is a little different from stress, anger, and regret. It is much less conscious and controllable. We can meditate on stress, use calmness to battle anger, and rationalize our way out of regret, but fear is another beast. When you are standing at the bank, the teller calls next, you come up to the thick plexiglass window and ask to withdraw all of your money for your startup, it's a scary feeling, and there is not much you can do about it. When you are 156,000 feet above the ground, and the door of the airplane opens and they say jump, you will be afraid — you just will be.

Anticipation of something that is painful, hurts. The longer you think about doing it, the more time you will spend anticipating, the scarier it will seem, and the harder it will be to take the first step.

We have all experienced something that we were afraid of. We thought about it, waited for the perfect moment, hoped it would come; it never came. We wished to get comfortable with the idea, but never did. We then thought, "Let me just wait." And so, we waited. But no matter how long the wait lasted, it felt just as scary. We just could not imagine ourselves doing it, it seemed impossible. The more we thought about it, the more uneasy it felt, and then we either just did it or we didn't.

It really came to one moment for most of us. It was when we felt the least ready, on the edge of uncertainty, our palms sweaty, the world against us, and we said ... fuck it. We tensed our jaw, focused, clenched inside, and just went for it. We took the leap into the unknown.

In that moment something happened. It wasn't just the adrenaline rush or the instant relief. It was something else. It was as if we stepped over the bar to the other side. What was before us, was now behind us. We almost entered another dimension, a place that we were wondering about for so long. We pondered how it would feel to be here. And then we pondered no more. We were there.

In that new space, there was no more fear. We felt like we regained stability. It was no longer the unknown. That leap could have even changed our perception of life and allowed us to see it a little differently. What we thought was impossible or unattainable, was now ours, in our hands. We felt less limited and more limitless.

I think a big portion of our life is about how many limitations we can overcome, and how quickly. Many people let fear truly limit them by, craftily burying them in their comfort zone where they continue wondering what it would have felt like to pursue their dreams.

They may wonder how it would be to kiss the girl they like, they may wonder how it would be to quit their job they hate, to be wealthy, or to be free. Hence, so many people continue living this limited life, wondering and never finding out. Unless one day, they just say fuck it and take a leap into the unknown.

We all know how that first step feels. It talks to you. It tells you why you should not do it. It tries to convince you that you are better off without it, because the risk is too great. It will craft these brilliant stories that will all make perfect sense.

This will go on until you just accept that fear is your biggest friend. It is an amazing teacher. It teaches us how to go after our dreams. It allows us to learn how to become comfortable feeling uncomfortable. When you are one on one with fear, that is when you learn the most about yourself. You learn what you are capable of and how much you can trust yourself to turn your wishes into accomplishments.

Nothing else so openheartedly gives you growth so that in return you have to give it love. **Love whatever scares you.** Fear is what forces you to step into the unknown territory where you feel vulnerable and fragile, and teaches you to OWN IT. Fear is the most loyal companion, it will never leave you. As long as you are alive conquering success, it will be by your side.

All you can do is welcome it, by re-wiring your brain's reaction to it by re-labeling the reason why we are experiencing this emotion. "I fear because I care," "I feel anxious because this is important to me," or "I am afraid because it is unknown." As simple as that.

We think we may be afraid for many different reasons. We may think we are afraid of the pain, failure, disappointment, disappointing others, loss, or even rejection. However, it is much simpler than that. We are afraid of the unknown.

If you knew how much pain you would experience if you fall, you would be ready to endure it. If you knew how hard something will be, you would not be afraid of not being able to take it. If you knew your business transaction would be a 100% success, you would invest readily — no hesitation, no fear. The problem is that you don't know.

When I was little, I loved Batman. When I got older, not a whole lot changed. I remember in the film, *The Dark Knight*, the Joker said, "If tomorrow I announce that a gang banger will be shot or a truckload of soldiers will be blown up … nobody panics. Because it's all 'part of the plan.' But when I say that one little old mayor will die, well then everybody loses their minds!"

There is so much truth to that, if something is expected, then we are okay with it, but if it is the unpredictable, unexpected, unknown, that throws people into panic and fear.

There are some extreme examples of this also. I had a client who was very unhappy, in lots of emotional pain and always distressed. She has been this way for almost fifteen years. The reason was because of the mental and physical abuse from her parents, that she withstood from an early age for almost two decades. At the time that we began our mentoring relationship, she had completely forgotten what it feels like to be happy, relaxed, and without pain. Those emotions were very unfamiliar to her. When I would ask her to imagine for even five seconds how it would feel to not be in pain, she would get very tense.

Being unhappy, in pain, and distressed felt comfortable because she had gotten used to it. It was all she knew. Although she still wanted to get out of that state on a conscious level, it felt scary subconsciously.

Until I figured this out, our progress was very slow. What was separating her from where she wanted to be, was anger, anger at her parents specifically. We tried several exercises to let go of the past. Yet I sensed that every time she tried, something was stopping her.

Then I realized that it's not that she couldn't let go of the past and stop being angry at her parents, which would finally make her feel happiness, appreciation, relief, and relaxation. She was afraid to let go. Those positive emotions were all so unknown to her at this point, that she was afraid to even experience them! She had no idea what feelings like that would bring her, and so she chose to be stuck in the familiar misery. At least when she was miserable, she knew what her days looked like, how it felt to wake up in the morning, how it was to deal with life.

What ultimately helped her, was not the techniques and exercises of letting go of her past, but rather familiarizing herself with her future. A future where she is happy, relaxed, relieved, and in love with life. We began doing visualization exercises where I would have her imagine those positive feelings, places she would go to while experiencing them, things she would do, and people she would see.

Little by little, she began to light up. The unknown was becoming more explored, she was becoming more comfortable with it, and once she began to feel the warm rays of her happier, brighter future, she let go of her anger at her parents.

This is the same concept of why people who are abused choose to stay in the abusive relationships. At least they know what to expect, it's familiar. Meanwhile, leaving the abuser opens an array of uncertainty and fear,

fear of the unknown. Where will they go, what is going to be there, how would it feel to be alone? So, many stay where they are.

The less you put yourself in the position where you have to overcome fear, the harder it becomes. It is just like everything else. If you stop doing pushups, they become harder, if you stop practicing calmness, it gets weaker. The good news, as always, is that the opposite is also true. Overcoming fear is just like training a muscle, the more you train it, the stronger it gets. The more of the unknown you overcome, the less scary stepping into it becomes.

For a woman, having her second child is less scary than having her first. For anybody, the third business is less scary to open than their second. And for a guy, the fourth girl he approaches is less scary than his third. Why? Not because people become braver, but because they already know what could happen!

Building the confidence to go into the unknown and familiarizing yourself with it as much as possible are two ways to battle fear. Yet, our human experience is so unique and creative. It crafts these cleverly designed situations that none of us could ever have predicted, and when we are most vulnerable, fires them at us. It is unforgiving. We can never know enough to eliminate all of the unknown, and so fear nothing. We need something more powerful.

Instead of trying to eliminate the unknown, or muscle through it with confidence, we can simply accept it, and embrace the journey! We fear because we are afraid that things will not go according to plan. Realistically, you will never know how things will work out. You can do everything right, and then some extenuating circumstance will come out of nowhere and fuck you.

Think about all of the natural disasters or epidemics, for example. Think about how all these business owners in Japan worked so hard in their enterprises, trying to make more money; think about all the workers who diligently executed their tasks, hoping to get promoted; think about all the plans everyone had. And then on March 11, 2011, a tsunami hit Japan and wiped out everything, including all of their plans. Who would have thought?

So, it is a little paradoxical that we fear the unknown because, in a way, everything is unknown. We resort back to probabilities of what could happen, to comfort ourselves. But in reality, we have no fucking idea what will happen tomorrow. **All we can do is live in a reality where there is no losing outcome. We must simply accept and embrace any outcome.**

We must accept any outcome as a winning outcome. Remember, what may seem as a curse today may turn out to be a blessing tomorrow. In the moment our knowledge is limited, our awareness is incomplete. We simply don't know if something is good or bad.

Life is like yin and yang. There is light and there is dark, there is black and there is white. Ups and downs are all part of our journey called life. The sooner we accept and embrace the journey, the easier it will be to live and overcome. Yet more importantly, we will cast away all fear of our expectations not being met, and will try new things unhesitatingly.

The last and final way to battle fear is through faith. My favorite slogan is, "If you have faith, you have no fear." It is faith in the Universe and the divine intelligence to take you where you need to be.

During the 2020 pandemic that shook the entire world, I talked to my friend who is a pastor at a Russian Orthodox Church, and I asked him, "Are you afraid to catch the virus?" He said, "No." I, of course, inquired, "How come?" His response was empowering. He said, "Because my faith in God is too strong, those who fear have no faith." He resumed his regular service, he saw people, he did everything as if the virus did not even exist. He was sixty-eight, and he made it through the pandemic just fine and so did everyone around him.

It's not that his faith made him immune to the virus, but not being in fear certainly helped. When one fears, their body goes into distress, the heart rate becomes incoherent, the blood flow slows down, more cortisol is produced, their vibrations lower, DNA contracts and their immune systems begin to suffer.[13] So they become more susceptible to any virus or infection.

---

[13] Rein, McCraty, "Structural Changes in Water and DNA Associated with New Philosophically Measurable States," *Journal of Scientific Exploration.*

Ultimately, it really comes down to what you want to do. Do you want to live paralyzed in fear or not? You can reduce your faith to an object that you believe keeps you safe, such as a bracelet or a neckless. As long as you wear it, you are untouchable. You can tell yourself any story you want, as long as it works for you.

Whether it is a business decision, a life decision, or just something dangerous, we have to first acknowledge that the reason we are not going for it is because we are afraid. Many people live in denial of this emotion, and so they can never understand why they are stuck in one place with time swiftly passing by them like a moving train that disappears in the fog of the future that they cannot attain. Try to finish this sentence for me, "If I wasn't afraid, I would…."

My friend Jeffrey always avoided fear, and lived a life full of comfort, until it buried him alive.

Chapter 11

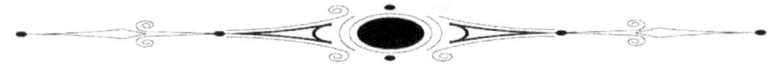

Jeffrey From the Box

For years, Jeffrey was stuck in a box. The box was soft, with plenty of space, and everything was right there conveniently at his fingertips. Years passed by, and Jeffrey began to notice something strange happening to his box. For some reason, oddly enough, it began to get smaller.

The walls narrowed, and Jeff didn't like it. He complained. He expressed how having less space was making him depressed and unhappy. He complained and complained, but the box didn't get bigger. Soon his skinny shoulders were touching the walls, he wasn't getting enough air, and he was tired of standing. To alleviate his weak little legs from the pain, so he sat down on the thin carboard bottom.

Jeff felt relief, his legs stopped hurting, and it felt much better, much more relaxing. When he lifted his head, something looked different. He saw that the small dot of light glimpsed between the four cardboard lid flaps seemed much further away now than before. He felt more trapped, but comfortable.

After sitting in one spot for several months, his back began to hurt, and so he decided to lay down. As his back flattened out on the floor of the box, Jeff felt relaxed, and his pain slowly withered away. He looked up once again and saw the same dot of light, his hope of escape, but this time it was even further away — so far, it felt unattainable. He accepted he would never reach it. Surprisingly enough, that thought felt relaxing in a way. All the sudden, he didn't have to try.

With time, he focused more on the walls of the box, and stopped looking up altogether. When he thought about escaping, he told himself, "That's not for me, my chance has passed." Over time, Jeffrey turned very pale, weak, and his blue eyes were fading into gray as he struggled to look up. Looking down was just easier. He grew old in this box.

One beautiful day, his dear friend Moses heard the news and ran to Jeffrey. He approached the box, and with one simple motion of his hand, opened the lid! The box immediately filled with sunlight, its brown walls lit up with positivity, everything became light, colorful, and there was Jeffrey.

He was laying on the ground, rotting inside the box. Moses picked him up with great difficulty because his body had begun to grow into the cardboard floor. As he lifted Jeffrey, his skin gained color, his skinny back straightened, and the sunrays entered his faded eyelids as he looked up at the blue, beautiful sky for the first time in years.

Moses was so happy, he was overwhelmed with joy that he opened the box for Jeffrey, and finally showed him the sky and the escape from these horrible four walls that he had been trapped in for so long. Moses shouted from excitement, "Jeff, you're free! The world is yours! You can do anything! You can be anyone! Climb out!"

To Moses' great surprise, confusion, and dismay, Jeffrey did not climb out. Instead, he looked back down at the cardboard floor, shrugged his shoulders, and slowly began to close the lids of the box back on himself, one by one.

Moses was shocked. He exclaimed, "Jeff, but why?!" Jeff replied, "Because I do not know what is outside the box. At least I know what is here, and here I am comfortable." He died in the box several days later; he weighed only fifty pounds.

When he knew he was dying, in the last hours of his life, all he felt was a tremendous amount of pain, pain of regret. Regret that he did not climb out of the box — and now it was too late.

Do you have a friend like Jeffrey?

The Foundational Realization

Throughout life, there are two paths we can take, to break out of the box, or never put ourselves in it in the first place. To break out of it, imagine that, unlike Jeffrey, you are an all-powerful, unstoppable being, who pounds on its walls with all of your strength and divine willpower, until you break through it, rupturing the wall with your fist, sliding both hands through the opening, and completely demolishing the entire box into shreds, along with all of its limitations. This ability comes from one foundational realization: that *we are the ones who create the box.*

We create it through our limiting beliefs. We then let these beliefs dictate who we are and what we are capable of, shadowing our dreams. We make self-limiting statements become our identity. If a person tells themself, "I am not a people person, I do not have what it takes to be wealthy, I do not have a business mind, I cannot get in shape, I cannot make myself do something, I cannot change my life," then realize that is the identity that the person creates for themself. They would look in the mirror and see just that, a socially awkward, poor, out-of-shape individual, with no power of will, and no way out. What kind of life is that person going to live?

These are all just beliefs! They come from no other place but our mind. We are the ones who construct the imaginary walls of self-restraint, reinforced by brilliant reasons of why we cannot do something. It is a fascinating concept — us limiting our success from within.

We consciously place ourselves in this box, and even chose how thick the walls will be. Some people have a whole series of invented notions that prevent them from living the life they want. "I cannot get a better job, because new workplaces give me anxiety, and that makes me feel worse about my self-image, which lowers my confidence, and that makes me not want to talk to people at all." To that man, that is his reality.

Yet everybody's reality is only real to them. It is a set of beliefs based on past experiences or experiences of others. So, even when that man will be guaranteed a better job through a referral, he will close the lid on himself and climb back into his miserable, low-paying hourly employment. One day, he will die with regret that he never took that chance while he could, and now it was too late.

It is harder to get out of the box than never place yourself in it. Unfortunately, we all experience this limiting self-talk to some extent. To avoid it, we just have to change our story. Many people's stories may be true, but they may not be serving them.

There was once a seventy-year-old man. Time took away his youth, and it was getting hard for him to walk up the stairs. He thought to himself, "I am too old to exercise." He rested more to alleviate the pain from his aching legs. As a result, his legs grew weaker. Soon he started to have a hard time even walking. He was stuck. He was losing strength, but he kept telling himself he was too old to get it back.

One day in the park, he saw a gentleman that seemed much older than him, jogging. In incredulity, he thought to himself, "He must have been jogging all his life." Coincidentally, a week later he saw the gentleman in a store. He approached him and explained that he had seen the other man jogging at a park and was very inspired. With great curiosity, he asked, "How long have you been jogging?" The gentleman replied, "I started last year." The first man could not believe the answer. His eyes widened and his eyebrows furrowed. Without hesitation, he asked, "What made you start?" The gentleman's look became distant, as if he remembered some deep feeling he once felt. After a short pause, he said, "When I was eighty, I started having trouble walking up the stairs. I felt like my body was getting weak. But I knew I wasn't too old to exercise, so I began strengthening my legs, and here I am."

The seventy-year-old man's face froze in an expression of disbelief. It was like he just witnessed something paranormal. In that single interaction, everything he believed in was discredited. He did not even share his problem; he thanked the gentleman and went home, to think about what just happened. He thought for hours, and then he realized that it is all about the story that you tell yourself.

What story are you telling yourself? Is it serving you? How much is your story helping you achieve your goals? You don't have to prove your story to anyone, it can be true all you want. Yes, it was true that the man was seventy and that he was old, there is not a single bit of falsity on that. Yet that truth was not helping him get back on his feet.

We can fall into a debilitating cycle that can only be ended by changing the story that starts it. For as long as that man tells himself that he is too old to exercise, he will grow weaker and weaker, while the other one will grow stronger and stronger. Say more things like, "I can do this, I will be successful at this, it's not too late." You will be surprised at how fast you and your body will respond.

The Easy Life

It is very easy to find a thousand reasons why we cannot do something. Why? Because then, we do not have to do it! We cleverly craft the box to keep us warm, comfy, and away from the demanding and difficult reality. We do not have to stress about possible failures, fear the uncertainty, or come out of our soft, fuzzy, comfort zones. It is so easy to not work out, all you have to do is just not go to the gym.

It is also very easy to be the victim. For victims, something out of their control always goes wrong, and now there is nothing they can do about it. So, they can just sit on their recliners with their legs up, complain about being a victim, and do nothing. I cannot tell you how many people I have heard blame being unemployed on bureaucracy. "There are no jobs … nobody is hiring … it's the government … the market" and so on, and so forth.

In September 2018, Tony Robbins came to Moscow for the first time. The reviews were horrible. They called him a scammer, that he did not say anything that they did not already know, and about everything else he was just wrong. I watched the entire presentation, and it was brilliant. I mean, truly life changing material, and this is coming from a life coach.

Yet, in Russia, a lot of people always complain about something. I realized that by discrediting Tony's presentation, they could just go home and do nothing. How easy! They do not have to implement what they learned, or try new approaches in life. As long as everything they just heard was bullshit, they are relieved from the effort of trying any of it. It shocked me how real this was.

There will be people who will read this book, and say, I knew all this already. Perfect, now they just excused themselves from having to change anything about their perspectives or their lives, and they could continue comfortably doing what they have been doing, and miraculously ending up in the same place with the same thing. **Victims avoid opportunity!**

We must avoid victim talk at all times, my friend. Coming up with excuses only makes us lose control over the situation. How many times in your life have you heard someone complain about a drinking spouse? Did they blame everything on that person? That he or she needs to get their life together, stop being an alcoholic, stop ruining their relationships with others, have sympathy for those around them who care, all the horrible things they do when they drink? Sounds familiar, right?

Notice something interesting: the person who complains, as long they are the victim of a drinking spouse, they are relieved of all responsibility. They don't have to do anything, because it's not them, it's the drinker. So, mountains of effort get lifted off their shoulders, and they can just sit back, relax, and continue being unhappy.

They would rather be happy, yes, but that requires effort. I always ask, "What have you done to break out of bad habits?" The answer I usually get is, "There is nothing that can be done." A typical victim-talk answer.

How about asking that person why do they do what they do? How about taking the time to understand that person's bad habit? Perhaps asking them how they feel? How about finding out what emotion they are repressing with their addiction?

In this world we try, we fail, we strive, we cry, but most of all, we live. In the easy life, we die unsatisfied, asking, "What have I done to deserve this?"

The book *Extreme Ownership*, by Jocko Willink, a retired United States Navy SEAL, has influenced me greatly. It talks about owning every single situation. Instead of blaming the world, labeling life as unfair, and think-ing about everything that is wrong right now, we take full responsibility. This does one thing: it makes us think about what WE can do differently, and that does something magical. It places the situation in our hands, and now, we can influence it.

Chapter 12

Henry the Millionaire

Henry was not born into a wealthy family. His father was a typist who worked very hard to provide for his family, and his mother worked at a bakery. Henry grew up hearing from both of his parents that hard work pays off. Unfortunately, Henry saw that his parents were often fighting because of money. It was always, "We don't have enough" and "We can't buy this, because we need to save," "We spent too much, and now we can't afford anything."

His father usually walked out of the room, with his head slightly down in accepting silence that this is just how things were. His mother usually looked hopelessly at the old, peeling, yellow lacquer layer of their wooden living room floor. Henry hated seeing his parents like this. He had this uncomfortable feeling of loneliness whenever they fought. He thought that if only his parents had more money, they would be happier.

Henry knew that he never wanted to live like this when he got older. He started working in a roofing company when he was sixteen. At the age of twenty-two, he started a roofing business himself. It was hard work, but every day he was crafting his strategy of submitting more bids, while polishing his skill with experience. Most importantly, he was making money.

He was motivated by his own progress to out-perform his competitors, spending late nights with a pencil between his teeth, and his tired eyes scanning the paperwork. He was carefully examining every opportunity. He loved it.

The next ten years were stressful, but exciting. On his parents' principles of hard work, Henry grew his roofing company and ended up selling it for two million dollars. His eyes widened, and he felt his pupils dilate with joy when he glanced at his bank account after selling his business. He thought to himself, that is too much money, and then laughed quietly.

Only later did he learn that too much money was not enough money. Nonetheless,

as a grateful son, he took care of his parents first. He bought them nice things, freed them from debt and made them proud. He bought himself whatever he wanted, too. It was like a dream come true, everything was great. He felt good when he acquired new things, so he got more. The more he got, the more he wanted. That is when things began to get a little complicated.

Henry had this weird anxiety develop over things he now owned. It was like the more he got, the more he had to lose. That paranoia began to grow its rotten roots deeper into his mind with every purchase. That didn't stop him, however. He bought more because at least in the moment of getting a new watch, a new bracelet, a new car, it made him feel good.

As the dopamine rush shortened, he began to explore other immediate little fulfillments. TV shows, video games, gambling, all for hours, sometimes days, as long as some external stimuli over-voiced the sound of emptiness inside. Henry began to eat, a lot. The more, the better, and if accompanied by some cognac, then it was the most perfect cancellation of the meaningless reality, even if just for a little while. That is how his bodily destruction in the name of happiness began.

One day, with a blank stare, he looked at his fifty thousand dollar watch that barely fit around his wrist anymore, and asked himself, "What happened to the times when I did not have all of this, and felt like myself?"

Henry thought about the times when he was building his business with sweat and hard work. He remembered those late nights, looking for new projects to bid on; he remembered how thrilling it was. Too bad that right now, it felt too monumental to do something like that again. His power of will weakened, and alcohol abuse strengthened.

He had too many emotions to repress, mainly guilt and shame, and alcohol just wasn't enough anymore. Henry started using drugs. He would pick up the phone and make a phone call to get a delivery.

It was winter all over again, with white mountains of happiness delivered, all in a bag straight to his door. The endless lines of comfort and instant gratification cast their seductive veil upon him, and it just made no sense to resist. As much as Henry knew this was not the way, the pain was too deep and the relief was so quick.

This was good for now. His world narrowed to a white, one-way street, meticulously crafted by a cold, single file blade on a silver plate. His body grew weak and his mind weaker. Nothing really mattered much anymore. It was all a chase, a constant, interminable chase, and he was running out of breath.

Henry thought to himself, how did he get here? It was such a blurred transition, and every wrong step he took felt so harmless. Only by looking in the mirror did he realize where he was now, but he had no idea how it happened. He was in denial. He was denying the direction of his journey, until he could no longer deny its destination. He overdosed.

It was a beautiful death, just like in the movies. Huge house, alone, on a soft, green leather couch, in a lavish red robe and blood endlessly running from his nose like a stream of consciousness.

At Henry's funeral, his parents were more miserable than ever. They talked about how he was a hard worker, just like they always taught him to be. They talked about how he was so self-disciplined, and how he constantly tried to grow and improve. His father spoke with pride about Henry's tremendous financial accomplishments and how he never forgot about his loved ones. As they lowered the body, his parents had it all, except for their only son.

A Slow Death

If you put a frog in hot water, it will jump out, but if you raise the temperature of mildly warm water slowly, it will boil to death. We are the same way, my friend. If someone had taken Henry when he just sold his business and showed him his reflection, and he saw in the mirror what he looked like before his death, he would have been struck. When we see our reflection every day, we don't really notice the change.

We do not notice how lack of movement kills us. We become less disciplined, less ambitious, lazy, we think slower, and eventually just lose the spark to life. It is a very slow death. Sometimes, it can literally kill us, like in Henry's case, which is a true story of someone my family knew.

It is a matter of repeated actions for the sake of empty good feelings that add up to meaningless lifestyles without purpose. Alcohol consumption, watching shows just for fun, or other activities that do not contribute to us physically, spiritually, or mentally, all seem harmless in the moment. Is it okay to do them occasionally? Yes.

The danger lies in something less obvious. It's not about the lost time that you could have used for something productive, it is about how hard it becomes to be productive. Your discipline becomes weak if you do not train it. The more we do not make ourselves do things that we need to, but may not want to do, the harder it is to be successful.

To some, losing weight could save their life, but they cannot make themselves work out, even when they know their life depends on it. It is the inability to turn their goals into accomplishments that slowly kills their dreams, and sometimes, kills even them.

Constant growth is not easy, being happy is not easy, and living a long, meaningful life is not easy. What is easy, is submitting to the vices, to the bodily pleasures, to the "I just want to relax," "I'll do it later," and "I do not feel like it." All of that amounts to the slow but progressive deterioration of our power of will, and without that, who are we? We are slaves. As Paramahansa Yogananda said, "Until you are a master of yourself, able to command yourself to do things that you should do but may not want to, you are not a free soul."

The water in the pot heats up for months, sometimes even years, before it begins to boil. Many homeless people, addicts, or overweight individuals did not become like that overnight. Their current state is a result of repeated actions. That is why it is crucial to be mindful of every action we take. Whenever we find ourselves falling into the habit of actions that do not advance us, we just have to become aware of that.

We die from comfort and lack of movement. Our body, brain, heart, nervous system, and our power of will, all grow stagnant if we do not challenge them. It becomes harder for us to accomplish goals, try new things, and more problems seem impossible to solve. Non-movement makes us deteriorate from the inside.

The water in the running river is clear because it is moving, and the water in the swamp is dirty because it is stationary. The bacteria blossoms where there is no movement. Similarly, diseases and mental sickness prospers in motionlessness.

Why can lack of movement be so detrimental to us? To answer that question, we have to understand some of the chemical activities of our brain. There is a biological reason to why people who set and accomplish goals regularly do not rely on empty habitual dopamine rushes that come from instant gratifications, like the ones Henry was chasing.

Dopamine is a neurotransmitter that helps control the brain's reward and pleasure centers.[14] It is "The Reward Molecule," and one of the neurochemicals contributing to us feeling good. The dopamine release tells the brain that whatever it just experienced is worth getting more of, because it felt good. That helps animals (including people) change their behaviors to attain more of the rewarding items or experiences.[15]

We can use this to our advantage endlessly. By setting goals and achieving them, the repetition of pursuing good-for-us rewards will build a new dopamine pathway in our brain, until it is robust enough to compete with a dopamine habit that we are better off without.[16] There is evidence that people with extraverted, or uninhibited, personality types tend to have higher levels of dopamine than people with introverted personalities.[17] So to feel good naturally, we can be more proactive in our daily lives by setting small goals and accomplishing them.

---

[14] Weaver, and Reppert, "Definition of the developmental transition from dopaminergic to photic regulation of c-*fos* gene expression in the rat suprachiasmatic nucleus," *Molecular Brain Research.*

[15] Brookshire, "Explainer: What is dopamine?" Science News for Students, January 17, 2017.

[16] 16. Loehr, The Only Way to Win, p. 4.

[17] Bergland, "The Neurochemicals of Happiness," Psychology Today blog, November 29, 2012.

This doesn't have to be anything crazy. I invite you to make a To Do List on your phone that ranges between things you want to get done today, this week, and this month. It can be anything work, health, or fun related. For example, do five pushups, update the work calendar, and go hiking at a new place you wanted to check out. Start small and build your way up.

Chapter 13

Your Mind is Not Your Friend

The truth is, our mind is not always our friend. Most of the time, we cannot trust it because it is designed to avoid pain. We were biologically made this way because it helped us survive even during the Stone Age. If something hurt, we knew not to do it because it could be dangerous to our lives. When we touched fire, we felt pain, so our brain told us that touching fire is bad and should be avoided. When we saw a saber tooth tiger, we felt fear, so our mind told us to run away because the tiger could kill us.

Fear hurts, stress hurts, uncertainty hurts, going outside your comfort zone hurts. So does waking up early in the morning, not eating after seven o'clock, starting to exercise or doing something new and challenging. It is all actual pain that your mind is experiencing and thus trying to avoid!

Our mind is quite selfish. It likes warmth, comfort, and doing what it is familiar with. Its job is to avoid pain in the form of stress, fear, and discomfort. It does not really care that you will rot on the filthy floor of a cardboard box, and die in misery; it cares about itself. There are two things you have to do to battle this.

First, we must separate from our mind. Your mind is not you. You are your spirit. When you die, your brain, with the rest of the body, will be buried, your soul will live because it is energy. Energy cannot be created or destroyed. It simply takes different forms.

So free yourself from your mind. It is just a tool used to help us survive, but not prosper. You may ask, but how can I do that? Understand the mind's motive. Listen to your mind very closely, and understand why it is saying what it is saying. When you sit down to study and you begin to procrastinate, your mind is saying, "Studying is pain, procrastination is pleasure, do what feels good." Every time you experience a moment like that, just reply, "No, I love the pain, pain is my pleasure."

Second, do not just love the pain, accept the pain! Accept that it will hurt. It has to hurt. Anything worth having is going to hurt, and that is great because pain makes us stronger, more durable, more bulletproof. Pain, just like fear, is growth. Prosperity and pain are inseparable. To welcome your prosperity, you have to welcome the pain.

Somebody once asked Arnold Schwarzenegger, "How did you achieve such stunning results in your fitness career?" He said, "It is all about the last two reps."

There is so much wisdom in those words. When your body is fuming from exhaustion, your muscles are ready to give out, and you feel like you cannot do any more, and in that moment, you do two more reps. Those two last reps will feel harder and more painful than the entire workout, but that is when your muscles grow the most.

You can train your mind the same way. It is taking that extra step, doing that one more thing, committing just a little more when you feel like you have done enough. That is what will put you in an unstoppable mindset, because that is exactly how you break through your limitations. Now that gives you something priceless — confidence. Confidence that you can do more than you thought, always.

Some clients I had, complained about how life seemed short and how time was passing by so quickly. Later, I realized one factor they all had in common. Their entire existence revolved around complaining about their life, and so they constantly tried to find the end to the pain. It was always about what can I do to be less in pain. Paradoxically, the more they tried, the more in pain they were. Eventually, they started going to a psychologist, then a therapist, and then finally decided to get a life coach.

With time, I recognized that it wasn't just some of my clients. Most people, I noticed, bend down to their mind. They spend most of their time making negative decisions — deciding which alternatives would be the least unpleasant, trying to keep things from getting worse. As time passes, such a person settles for less and less, because in their mind, they are avoiding what hurts. They start believing that it isn't possible to be free and profoundly happy. When you tell them there are ways to break out of their pattern, all they can see is that to do so would take more effort, and thus cause more pain.

With time, they shorten their stick, until they eventually run out. Each time you avoid immediate pain and do what feels good in the moment, you think you are escaping a difficult price, while in reality, you will only be paying a bigger one.

My aunt used to be a great example. I was still a kid at that time. She used to be overweight. Every time we told her to eat healthier or to eat less, she would refuse. To her, food was everything and giving that up was too unpleasant. She continued gaining weight. Her cholesterol went up, and she started having blood pressure problems.

We told her to do go for regular walks outside. She never had trouble walking, yet because of her unwillingness to eat less, walking began to increase her heart rate and she would experience shortness of breath. She was in pain. She continued not being active. At least, that didn't cause her any more pain.

She began to develop arthritis because of the tremendous pressure on her joints due to excessive weight. We told her she should do other exercises that didn't involve walking. She refused, because although it wasn't physically painful, forcing herself to get up and do them was stressful enough. Doing nothing was just easier. Her pain got worse.

Soon, she was not able to get out of bed and spent the majority of her time in deep depression. She finally achieved her goal, there was no more pain to avoid, because her whole life has become mere suffering. She was in physical and emotional pain from the moment she woke up to the moment she medicated herself to sleep. I was too young to help her.

Another reason why our mind is not our friend is because of the negative bias in our brain. It is the brain's tendency to focus more on the negative than the positive. Dr. Rick Hanson, a neuroscientist and author of the *Buddha's Brain,* explains negative bias, "Negative stimuli produce more neural activity than do equally intensive positive ones. They are also perceived more easily and quickly."[18]

So, it is not only more neurologically stimulating to think negatively, it is also easier! The reason why this is dangerous, is because repetition is the mother of all learning. When we repeatedly think negatively, we are firing and re-firing the same neurons responsible for the negative bias. This is how pessimistic people become pessimistic, they are not born this way.

Have you ever heard an expression that a person can get used to anything? Maybe you have experienced this yourself. When you observe someone do something very demanding or straining, you ask yourself, "How can they be okay with this?" Yet surely enough, one day you find yourself in their position doing the same thing, but being okay with it.

I remember when I went to live in Russia for half a year, I could not understand how people put up with public transportation there in the winter. It seemed like the most daunting, painful, and beyond inconvenient experience.

You had to stand at a bus stop for thirty-plus minutes in freezing cold. Once on the bus, now you were hot because of all the clothes, so you had to undress. This whole time you have to hold your hat, gloves, and scarf in your hands. Your shoes are constantly destroyed and wet because of all the melted snow mixed with mud.

It just all seemed like the last thing I could picture myself ever getting used to, and yet, sure enough, after living there for two months, I did not mind any of this at all. It seemed completely normal to me.

The reason I am saying all this, is because the wiring of our brain is not static, it is not irrevocably fixed. Our brain is adaptable. Neuroscientists discovered that our brain can develop new patterns, new combinations of nerve cells and neurotransmitters in response to new inputs, new thoughts, experiences, and changes of perspective. This is what neuroplasticity is all about.

---

[18] Hanson, "Confronting the Negativity Bias."

Therefore, we are able to re-wire our brain to stop self-sabotaging or thinking negative thoughts that ruin our day, and eventually our lives. In the Chapter about meditation, we talked about how to distinguish between facts and beliefs; **That no matter how right we may think we are, if it is a belief, then it is based on assumptions, and therefore could be completely wrong.** Why? Because we simply don't know unless there is independently verifiable evidence. Let's go further with that idea.

Before, I thought we had control over our thoughts. Through numerous failures, I realized it is impossible. Especially with all the mental tricks our mind plays on us, as you can now see. The only thing we can control is our perspective, which then changes our belief.

You see the world the way you see it because of your perspective of it. Have your perspectives about anything ever changed? When you thought the reason to something was one thing, but it turned out to be something else? Did this happen when you finally found out something you didn't know before? And better yet, something you had absolutely no way of knowing?

Have you considered that if one of your perspectives was wrong, then ALL of your perspectives are wrong? And since they make up your reality, then your reality is not actually what we perceive it to be? Can you imagine that? That everything that you had an opinion about, everything that you believed, every reason why you thought someone didn't like you, every reason why you thought someone did something, every intention that someone had, every story you told yourself, could ALL be false.

Maybe not all, but which ones are true and which ones are false? We may never really know. Due to the negative bias of our brain, most of the time our mind tells us to believe the negative more, because it is more neurologically stimulating, and it is perceived more easily and quickly.

Personally, the question that will never leave me, is how much energy and happiness have I wasted living a reality that turned out to be false? Next time you experience a thought that sends you into believing something that makes you feel uneasy or sad, no matter how true you may think it is, unless it is a fact, just remember, **you're not always right, my friend.**

You can construct a reality that makes you experience peace and happiness, and it may be true or false. Or you can construct a reality that makes you experience pain and misery; it may be true or false. Just like our earlier example about the driver who cut you off when he was rushing to the hospital. That might have been true or false. The bigger question is, which reality brings you more peace? The reality you chose to live is your choice! **So, start living as if the ultimate reality that makes you happy IS the reality!** Meanwhile, remember, your mind is not your friend.

To finish this chapter off, I want to say, don't stress about making tremendous changes in your life. A large portion of this book is designed to simply bring you awareness to what is going on inside of you. View this book as a toolkit that helps you observe your thoughts, feelings, and ultimately, your life.

I want you to first understand why do the things that happen, happen? Either way, you can't fix a problem unless you are aware of it, just as how a mechanic can't fix your car until he figures out what's wrong with it. When you have more knowledge and awareness, the rest will follow.

Chapter 14

Casting Out All Doubt

I've noticed in the last five years, there has been this whole movement about the power of belief. If you believe in something strongly enough, it will happen. At first, it was centered around the entrepreneur community. It was combined with positive thinking, and that all of your dreams will come true.

Then the power of belief transitioned into healing. That in order to heal a person, you need to believe in their healing, and they will be healed. The best part was that if the person didn't get healed or what you believed in didn't happen, well then you just didn't believe in it strongly enough.

I looked at all of this and thought, something is missing from this picture. I was right, what was missing was my understanding of why everyone was doubling down on the whole concept of believing. What helped me see the deeper meaning, was looking to the other side.

Imagine if you wanted to be successful in your next business venture, but all you thought about was how you failed at a previous one, how you will probably fail again, and how you really don't have what it takes. Imagine if you decided to study reiki, began healing a person, and all you thought about was how this isn't going to work, and that they will never heal. Imagine if you were planning to run a marathon, but you kept thinking how you are not capable, how your heart may stop, and how you will probably never finish it even if you tried.

How likely are you to become successful in your business, heal that someone, or finish a marathon?

What is one word that can describe the state of mind that causes one to think what I described in all three of these examples? Doubt. This is not about some magical power of belief; it is not about you not accomplishing something because you didn't believe hard enough; it is about staying away from doubt. Because doubt will always take us further away from that what we set out to do.

Don't confuse this with damage control. Calculating the risk that we simply have to be aware of, and knowing how to mitigate if it happens, is crucial. It is being ready for the worst, and knowing what to do if it happens, but not anticipating it. Remember, where your attention goes, your energy flows. Be mindful of your energy. Don't let more of it flow to the likelihood of failure rather than the possibility of success.

Think about how you feel when you start constructing schemes of negative self-talk in your mind. What happens when you begin to doubt yourself, your success, or your abilities? Does it give you more hope? Does it motivate you? Does it give you more desire and energy to try? Does it help you accomplish the goal faster? Then what is the point of doubting?!

I know it's not as easy to just cast out all doubt, but understand that there is a reason why successful people become more successful, and unsuccessful people become more unsuccessful.

Let's take two men, Frank and Tom. For the sake of the example, let's assume that they both are in the same city, have the same amount of money, and overall are in an identical situation across the board. Both decide to pursue their next business idea.

Frank says, "I really want to do this, but there is a lot of competition. I'm not really sure if it will work, many tried and many failed." He goes for it, but because of his doubts, he feels less motivation, less driven, and less enthusiastic. This makes him put less of his energy and effort into the project. The commitment is just not there. As a result, he ends up with a bad outcome.

That bad outcome reinforces his initial doubtful thoughts. He says, "I knew this wasn't going to work, and I was right." Next time he sets out to do something, he will tell himself, "Well, that previous thing didn't work, so this one probably won't either." His confidence in his abilities decreases, and his doubt in himself accumulates. That takes him further away from even trying his next big idea, and closer to just wondering about it forever.

Tom, on the other hand, says, "There may be a lot of competition, many tried and many failed, but I believe in myself. I believe in my vision, and I believe in my success." In this powerful, unstoppable mindset, Tom feels driven, motivated, and enthusiastic. This makes him put in the maximum amount of energy, maximum amount of effort, and maximum amount of time. There is full commitment. As result, he ends up with a good outcome.

This good outcome reinforces his initial belief. He tells himself, "I knew I could do it, and I did it!" Next time he sets out to do something, Tom will tell himself, "If I did that thing, I can do this thing." That makes him approach his next project with even less doubt and more confidence, yielding better results.

What is happening, is that people who become more successful strengthen their dopamine pathways, and through constant serotonin releases become more confident in their abilities. So, conquering new heights becomes easier for them. It is a dopamine-serotonin loop. The more confidant we feel in our abilities, the more eager we are to pursue a goal and give it our best. We approach the situation positively because we believe that if we achieved all the things prior to this one, then we will probably be successful at this one too, even if it is harder.

Actually, a variety of popular anti-depressants are called Serotonin-Specific Reuptake Inhibitors (SSRIs). SSRIs usually take a couple weeks to start working, because their effect has to do with neurogenesis, which is the growth of new neurons. [19] This is why over time, the more goals we achieve, the more neurons we grow, the easier it becomes to achieve new goals. Hence, successful people usually become more successful. The opposite is also true.

The more goals we set and the more of them we accomplish, the more self-esteem we build. We become more confident in our abilities, and that makes more things seem possible. "If I was able to do that, then I

---

[19] Bergland, "The Neurochemicals of Happiness."

can do this," is what we will hear ourselves say more often. Over time, saying "I did it!" more will produce a feedback loop that will reinforce behaviors that build positive self-image, make us less insecure, and create an upward spiral of more serotonin. [20]

As the dopamine-serotonin loop can get stronger, it can also get weaker, like in Frank's case. Where does this vicious downward cycle begin? IN OUR DOUBTFUL THOUGHTS! This is partially why they call it the *power of belief.* It is the power of avoiding a downward path of doubt leading to forgotten dreams.

Of course, life happens, and we will never always win. Yes, not having something go our way can humble us, and perhaps even make us doubt ourselves next time around, but that's okay. As long as we learn from our mistakes and adapt.

I wanted to create a digital art gallery. I found the space, spent ten thousand dollars on equipment, got a logo done, website, everything. Then the pandemic hit, and all forms of indoor entertainment got restricted. My plan came crashing down. This definitely put a dent in my confidence about the success of the whole project. What was worse, I was already heavily invested in it.

I told myself if I can't have the gallery in real life, I will have it in virtual reality. I bought Oculus Quest, and began mastering Google Tilt Brush. In one month, I created a twelve hundred square foot virtual reality gallery space that had a twenty-five-foot-long couch in a form of a pagoda, a giant twenty-six-foot-wide screen in front of it, and five sacred rooms. Each room was dedicated to a different religion; Christianity, Buddhism, Islam, Judaism, and Hinduism, and a self-realization fellowship shrine symbol on top of all of them, because self-realization recognizes and bows to saints of all religions. It turned out really nice.

In this gallery, I put up different messages on walls that encompassed what I teach, and actually many things that I write about in this book. It became a virtual reality gallery spiritual temple. The only problem was, that I had nowhere to show this to people. I once again felt a little trumped by that.

---

[20] Bergland, "The Neurochemicals of Happiness."

Simultaneously, at my penthouse, I began experimenting with an Augmented Reality projector. Soon, I created an augmented reality twenty-three-minute art show, with very powerful spiritual messages inserted into it. Then I realized, I will just show my virtual reality gallery in my house, combined with the augmented reality show!

It turned out that nobody has ever done this before, so I became the guy who created the world's first augmented / virtual reality gallery. My tickets were ten dollars per person. However, because of the CDC regulations, I couldn't have a lot of people come see it all at once in a day. This once again affected my confidence in the whole idea.

I decided to play on the exclusivity aspect, and made it only one tour for two people once a day, for one hundred and forty dollars. It became sold out every day for weeks. I was very happy about that. This is how the Double Reality Gallery was born, as a result of several failures.

Yes, not everyone who believes in their success is successful, but for what reason? I had many business ideas that never saw the light of the day. However, that was because I gave it my best and then saw that the model wasn't working, so I either dropped it or changed it. I learned and readjusted my direction. **Casting doubt is all about not diminishing your commitment when you approach a new obstacle.**

The work of Norman Doidge, a Canadian-born psychiatrist and the author of the book *The Brain That Changes Itself* indicates, "Harmful behavior, if allowed to loop in the brain continuously, will inevitably alter thought processes. Altered thoughts lead to altered beliefs which lead to a change in behavior and that is how you become a different person."[21] **So, there is a relationship between our thoughts and structural changes in our brain.** This further explains why unsuccessful people become more unsuccessful with time.

Doubt also leads to a decrease in neuroplasticity, which surprisingly shuts down your dreams of achievements, and here is why. Norman Doidge explains that the term "neuroplasticity" describes lasting change to the brain throughout the person's life. Through neuroplasticity, we can increase our intelligence and our emotional intelligence; we can

---

[21] Runwonder "2018 Science Explains What Happens to Someone's Brain From Complaining Every Day."

learn life-changing skills; and we can learn and unlearn harmful behaviors, beliefs, and habits.

If we repeatedly think that we are incapable of achieving something, our neuroplasticity decreases, and it becomes harder to live a free life. We get stuck in limiting beliefs and habits that get us nowhere. As a result, we change as a person for the worse. This is what we witnessed happening to Frank. This is why it is so crucial to set new goals, cast out all doubt, and strive to accomplish our goals.

Now the biggest question: HOW do we cast out all doubt? It is, of course, easy to say just focus on the positive and close your eyes on all the negative. During my consulting practice, I found it fascinating how differently this part was received and implemented by every client. For some, it was just a matter of telling them to cast out all doubt away when they doubted a particular outcome. Just that one simple phrase was enough. For others, not so much.

With practice, I realized that this phrase has to be said at the right time to be effective. It has to be done when you are experiencing doubt. Otherwise, it is just a phrase. However, for that to happen, we first have to do something that you have been reading endlessly about in this book — we have to become aware of our doubtful thoughts!

This is the hardest part because many people are so used to doubting themselves or their dreams that they stopped noticing it. It is just a way of life for them. "I will probably not get it," or "Most like it will not happen." How many times have you caught yourself saying that without paying much attention to it? That's a tricky question, I know.

Doubt combined with the negative bias of our brain, and the negative thoughts being more neurologically stimulating (as you read earlier), becomes a dangerous cocktail. If we also mix some law of attraction in there, that we attract that which we think and feel, then it can really result in everlasting unsuccess.

However, you see, it all starts with awareness. Next time you experience uncertainty about yourself or an outcome, just become aware of it. Don't do anything else, just simply catch yourself doubting.

Once you do, here comes your moment, the magical phrase that you soon will not be able to live without, your new mantra that should become engraved in your mind and triggered during times of uncertainty, just say, "I CAST OUT ALL DOUBT."

If that doesn't work, then let's dig a little deeper and find out why. Perhaps you are starting to realize why the chapter about fear comes before your mind not being your friend and that chapter comes before this one.

Who is doubting you? Is it you or is it your mind? Remember, your mind is not you, your spirit is you. Could it be that your mind is just playing games on you? Is there a possibility that it is cleverly crafting reasons for you not to do something, because it is trying to prevent you from experiencing fear of the unknown, the pain of forcing yourself to do something for the first time, or the discomfort of trying?

Fear of the unknown will always be there, and your mind will do everything in its power to avoid it. It will send you doubtful thoughts, just so that you wouldn't try. It will give you all the reasons why you can't and shouldn't do it.

The fear will knock on your door many times, and your mind will answer. Your mind will say, "Sorry, but I'm not sure about all this, I think you have the wrong house." Then the fear, that is your dear friend, will look down sadly and walk away from your door forlornly, knowing that it failed to give you the gift of growth and advancement.

Become aware of that. Don't fall for the sleazy little tactics of your mind. It is not your friend.

The Shift

The biggest shift in your life will happen when you turn from a doubting mentality to a knowing mentality. When we live knowing, we succeed. We also attract more of that what we want. We are able to build an all-powerful, divine charge that takes us where we need to be. We become truly unstoppable because there is nothing interrupting our flow.

When we live knowing, we shut down the inner dialogue full of doubt. Train your internal voice to say, "I know I will get what I want, and absolutely nothing and no one will stop me." However, don't forget, your will must coincide with God's will. If you set out to destroy this planet, or do bad to others with a mentality of "I will get what I want and absolutely nothing will stop me," you will face plenty of difficulties and obstacles along the way. Ask yourself, "**Would God want me to do this?**"

Living knowing is not blindly believing the impossible, it is simply a way to counter doubtful thoughts. Now, that is absolutely the most essential ingredient for the next part of this book. I need you to enter it having cast out all doubt.

Chapter 15

Change Your Energy, Change Your Life

Growing up and into my adulthood, I always had this notion that our thoughts somehow materialize themselves. I mostly found evidence of that, when I expected something bad to happen and it would. For some reason, very rarely did this work the opposite way. I couldn't understand how it happened or what was causing it. I just knew I should stay away from negative thoughts as much as possible.

I believe I was about seventeen when I began to be conscious of my thoughts. This is where my journey of positivity began. Yet, I wasn't so much interested in bringing good things into my life as much as I wanted to do everything possible to avoid bad ones from happening. It worked on a small scale, but I still got hit with some big hardships.

They included endless moving violations, losing my phone, car accidents, breakups, and much more. It all took a toll on me and my positive thinking. At some point, I just accepted the hardships as being part of life and there was nothing I could do about them. I felt helpless.

This notion of thoughts materializing into reality continued, but I still could not explain it. I just carried through life noticing evidence of it, but still could not explain it.

My one friend, who was thirty-eight at that time, has been single for eight years. He desperately wanted to get a girlfriend and eventually get married. However, he kept on constantly saying that there were no good girls in Los Angeles. The more women he met, the more disappointed he became.

He was stuck in this loop where he believed there were no good girls, so he kept on meeting all these girls that were just like that, which reinforced his initial belief. After enough of these cycles, he lost all hope, and just retracted all of his efforts. Loneliness was swallowing him up, and so he grew resentful toward all women. He became very unpleasant to hang out with. At that time, unfortunately, I couldn't help him.

I did however ask him, "So, what is a good girl?" He went on with his elaborate description of his perfect woman. I thought to myself, I have met plenty of girls like that in LA, but I didn't say it, because it would infuriate him. I then asked him, "What do you think your chances are of finding a girl like that here?" He said, "Absolutely none." I just looked at him with my eyes wide open, trying my best not to scream out, "But you are so fucking blind! They are everywhere!"

We were literally living in the same city, the same neighborhood, going to the same parks and places. The interesting thing was that we never picked up girls together, because it just felt very uncomfortable. I remember the drive from his house that day very vividly, because I felt like an animal trapped in a cage, beating on its walls trying to understand this paradox.

That was when I was suddenly enlightened with a realization. I exclaimed to myself, "What you expect is what you attract!" It was still far from the full picture, but I now had something to work with. I had a theory to test out, but ironically, I was the one who was doing everything wrong.

When I moved to Los Angeles, several people told me that people in LA are insincere and are not very friendly. For two years, I could not make any good friends. Even in my law school, I found my classmates to be self-absorbed and unapproachable.

I then met this one guy at a park where they had pull-up bars and parallel bars. He was doing calisthenics, which I had gotten into a few months earlier at that time. It turned out he had moved here only five months earlier himself, from Michigan. I told him I was from out of state also, and so we clicked.

We started talking, and I just could not help but share my unfriendly experience in LA so far. He looked at me, puzzled, and replied, "Really? Everyone in Cali is so chill and friendly." I was taken back. It was so opposite from what I believed and experienced, that it was actually a somewhat surreal moment for me. It felt like someone just told me, "Hey, man, yeah, I can levitate, it's no problem." He then said, "Yeah, come to Venice on Sunday. I will introduce you to some of my friends."

I did just that. I got there exactly on time. Until the very last minute, I thought the guy was just delusional. I thought I would show up there, he would point to a group of strangers who didn't know him, and be like, "Meet my friends." I was wrong.

There were almost twenty people there, and they were all his actual friends. I was genuinely surprised at how laid back and friendly they all were. I felt very welcomed, and that day we all trained calisthenics together. We talked about the sport, motivation, and life in general. I was able to build a close connection with them, something I have not experienced for two years at that time. The next Sunday, we all met up again.

I went from no friends to twenty in one day. But more importantly, I went from thinking it's impossible to find real down-to-earth people in LA, to finding a whole group. Yet, when I went back to school, that was when the true magic happened.

I remember walking into my Evidence class, and two guys, that always sat together in a row in front of me, started talking to me and invited me to study with them. I was a bit surprised, because I did nothing to even initiate that conversation. Meanwhile, we were in the same class for over six weeks already.

That week, the entire school changed right before my eyes. I began talking to people in the kitchen, in the library. I started exchanging outlines and learning people's names. They were all the same people that I spent two years with! Nothing had changed. Same school, same building, same individuals, but everything was different now. It was like everyone collectively took their masks off, and for the first time, I saw their true identity. However, it was really ME who took his mask off.

I began to explain this to myself using the limited knowledge that I had. It made sense that other people may sense us. For my friend, whenever he talked to a new girl, she sensed his prior dissatisfaction with women and him thinking, "She's probably just like all others." Not only would he not give a poor girl a chance, she might have even mirrored his emotions and became arrogant toward him.

For me, because I expected people to not care, my body language might have communicated that. I might not have been as present, or listened as carefully to them, because I figured, "Well, they do not care anyway." Yet, then I might have been the one who appeared indifferent, which pushed them back.

Now that I look back at this, that was a very nearsighted explanation. I was just scratching the surface. I did have one big clue at that time that helped me take my understanding a bit further.

I became interested to learn all religions, so I began studying Buddhism. In *Heart Sutra* of the Mahayana Buddhism it says, "Reality exists where the mind creates a focus." In other words, where our attention goes our energy flows.

If our attention settles on the misfortunate present, that is where we are sending our energy; it is all we see, and that becomes our reality. If our attention goes on the expectation of failure, or disappointment in our future social relationships, that is where we are sending our energy; it is all we see, and that becomes our reality. If our attention goes on the corrupt aspects of any government, that is where we are sending our energy; it is all we see, and that becomes our reality.

For me, my attention was always on how people in LA were insincere and not friendly. I talked about it, I told others about it, and most of all, I believed it. As a result, this is what I saw in the majority of people I encountered. I even misinterpreted many people's behavior, now that I think back, because that's all my attention was on — that everyone in LA was unapproachable and self-absorbed. That was my reality. And it felt very real. So real, I didn't make any friends for two years.

What does all that you have already come across in this book look like? So far, we learned that reality is based on perspective, perspective is based on beliefs, beliefs are made out of assumptions, and assumptions arise out of where we place our attention and focus! To shorten this, "Reality exists where the mind creates a focus."

As you can see from my personal example above (and I can give thousands more), once I changed my perspective, I changed my reality. You can explain that how I explained it to myself when I was twenty-four, or how I am explaining it to you now, the choice is yours. Yet the universal explanation lies in one word — energy.

My own first life coach that I hired once told me, "If you want to change your life, you have to first change yourself." She was right, but what exactly is it that I had to change about myself? With years, I found the answer to my question. **If you want to change your life, you have to first change your energy!**

Chapter 16

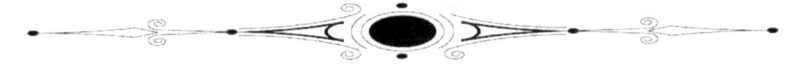

How to Change Your Energy

This chapter is where the magic begins. Now that we know how to minimize the presence of negative emotions that slow us down, such as stress, anger, doubt, and regret, it is now time to step into the simplest, most effective methods that will get you extraordinary results with ease, and allow you to unlock your limitlessness.

Up until I came to this realization at the age of twenty-seven, I always worked very hard, but I didn't get very far. There was a time when I failed the California Bar exam, quit my job, subleased my tiny studio, and moved to Russia for half a year. That is where I started writing my second draft of this book. Ironically, the title at that time was *Ease Your Life and Become the Best That You Can Be.*

I feel like I came up with that title subconsciously because deep down I knew that there was no way I was putting in so much hard work and still not getting anywhere close to where I wanted to be. I wanted things to get easier. It is so interesting that I sensed the solution to my problem, yet had no idea how to solve it.

I always had a list of goals and deadlines and actionable steps I needed to take to accomplish them. I even already lived by the philosophy of "Expect nothing and try everything," which reduced the stress but did not increase my results. I didn't know what it was, but I knew two things for sure, there was definitely something I should have been doing that I wasn't, and something I shouldn't have been doing that I was.

The minute I tell you what goes in each one of those two categories, it will all make sense! You will understand why you are where you are, you have what you have, and don't have what you don't have. It may differ in many ways, but one thing I promise you, everything is very simple.

One of my favorite movies is *The Butterfly Effect*. The movie is about how just one action or one decision can sometimes put you on a different trajectory in life, and lead you to a different outcome. It can lead you to being a different person, being with a different partner, living in a different place, and so on. The main character, Evan Treborn, has an ability to go back in time, and when he does, he takes a different action at a particular moment and that leads him to a different outcome in the future.

It is interesting that at the time when he is about to make a different decision, that will take him to a different reality in life, that reality already exists as a quantum possibility. The reason why this movie remains my all-time favorite is because it mimics our life perfectly.

Let's dive into some terminology. What do I mean by quantum possibility? It is a possibility of something happening. The quantum field of energy is the electromagnetic field of energy that exists all around us and in us. I use "quantum possibility" and "electromagnetic potential" synonymously because they represent the same thing, so don't get thrown off.

Now, different variations of our future, just like in *The Butterfly Effect*, already exist as quantum possibilities. There is a quantum possibility of you being rich and of you being poor, you finding love and not finding love, you getting a job and not getting a job. This means that the future we desire already exists as electromagnetic potential. Us finding our soul mate, or making millions, is a possibility that potentially ALREADY happened and exists as information that we can tap into.

There is already that day when you bring a suitcase full of money home, open it, and toss hundred dollar bills up and watch them rain. Watch how they are slowly landing right before you, and you sit in this pile of cash, laughing, enjoying the exhilarating feeling that it gives you.

That day already happened in the quantum of possibilities, because, why not? Why can't that be a possibility?

Imagine there is already a day when you are walking, holding the hand of the woman you love, as you both watch the sunset and you see how the color of her eyes gets highlighted by the sun rays when she looks into yours and tells you she loves you. You feel content with life, excited about the future, and satisfied with the present. Why can't that exist in the realm of possibilities? Why can't this be a potential outcome of your love life? Why not?

To contrast, if I asked you to imagine growing a pair of wings and flying away, that's not possible. So that probably doesn't exist as an electromagnetic potential in the quantum field of possibilities.

The question is, what do you want? Do you want to be healthy, wealthy, solve a problem, find a romantic relationship, or have a mystical experience? I will tell you something, not only those potentials of your bright, wonderful, warm, desired future are literally already there, they are waiting for you! So, what's the holdup?

It is us, continuously thinking about what it is and what it has always been. It is the constant acknowledgment of where we are now and where we want to be. This may seem counterintuitive at first. If we want to be wealthier, we say, "I want more money," which sounds good. We are identifying what we want and voicing our desire to get it. What's wrong with that?

Yet in reality, what's happening is that you are acknowledging what it is right now. That is, you not having the amount of money you want. Think about this, "I want more money": how does acknowledging not having the amount of money you want to have right now make you feel? Perhaps, a feeling of lack, or even frustration, or sadness?

Experiencing those emotions makes you tap into them, and become a vibrational match to other things that make you feel this way. One thing is certain, you are definitely becoming a vibrational match to the possibility of not having more money.

Don't forget: where your attention goes, your energy flows, and reality exists where the mind creates focus. If you are constantly saying, "I want more money," your attention is on not having it now. Accordingly, the reality that continues to exist is the one where the mind creates focus

— you not having enough financial freedom. Moreover, now you are attracting that quantum possibility into your future, so you continue to lack having more money.

Another example is if we say, "I'm tired of being sick." Sounds great, your wish is my command, but no. In that moment, you are underlining what it has always been. That is, you not having the health you want. How do you feel in that moment when you say that? Do you feel happy, relieved, and excited? Through your feelings, you align yourself with the corresponding quantum possibility — more illnesses.

In both instances, your thoughts are on what it is and what it has always been, not on what you want. You are focusing on the lack and the absence of that what you wish for. Why would you do that? If you really want something, why not focus on having it, rather than not having it?

This is the holdup. It is in not thinking thoughts that correspond with your desires. As long as we do that, we cannot become a vibrational match to the wealth, health, peace, love, and happiness we request. Your focus is elsewhere. Only once you align your intention, attention, and feelings with that what you want, can you absorb it into your present space and time reality. When we do that, everything begins happening with ease, and we don't have to work as hard anymore, because we step on the path of least resistance.

To make this work, you will need the three components at the same time: intention, attention, and feeling. If you are missing even one of the three, don't expect the magic to work.

Step 1 — Intention

This is the very first step in accomplishing your goals — forming a clear intention. To get what you want, you need to first identify what it is. As a life coach, I often ask people what they want. Many give me these vague answers, like 'I want to be successful' or 'I want peace'. When I ask them, "What would that look like?" I often get blank stares.

A lot of people fail at the very first step. Without forming a clear picture of the event that they want to achieve or manifest, there is no foundation to build on. If you can't imagine the future that you desire, then there is nothing to work toward. What is your destination?

Without a well-defined intention, everything else you are about to read would be like holding the most sophisticated GPS, but not having an address to put into it. Where can you expect it to take you?

Right now, think of a goal that you have in mind. Take out a flashcard and write the first letter of that goal on the front of it. For love you can put "L," for a new house you can put "H." Describe it to yourself in great detail. Pretend you are describing a painting you want an artist to create or a movie scene that you want a producer to film.

If you want a new job, imagine your workday there. What you do, how big your office is, what is on the walls, what your relationship with your co-workers is, how your boss treats you, what are some of your daily duties, and so on. Make it as real as possible. as if you are actually already experiencing it.

If you want a romantic relationship, imagine events associated with it. As you imagine a date with that person, for example, think about some of the character traits you see in that person, physical attributes, what do you enjoy about them, what does that person do, how does that person treat you, what are some things that person says to you, and so on. Describe them as if you wake up in the morning next to him or her, and go through your day having him or her in your life.

If you want more money, imagine events associated with that. The things you would do with it, you going to different places, buying different things, eating at nice restaurants, staying at fancy Airbnbs, contributing to causes, positively influencing lives, giving people hope, making a difference. Notice these are all logistics, don't worry about how you would feel just yet.

If somebody asked you about your current job, or your current romantic relationship, notice how you would easily be able to answer all of these questions and more, because you are already experiencing it. This is a level of detail you need to have with your imagination. Make the details whatever you want them to be. Don't worry about it being right, wrong, possible, or impossible. Have fun with the ideas. Watch these events as if you are watching a movie.

I warn you, the only things you are not to imagine are **how** it will happen, **when** it will happen, and **where** it will happen. I will explain to you why later.

We still have to put the work in; that is a given. On the back of the card, write actionable steps you would need to take to accomplish your goal, with deadlines attached to each step. If you don't meet the deadline, it's okay, just set a new one. Notice that if you don't have a clear intention, then it would be very hard to even make a list of actionable steps that will take you there.

This is exactly why casting all doubt was the grand finale chapter before I let you in on all of this. If you doubt having the future you want, you can't form a clear intention, and our Step One will be missing. My friend might have had a good idea of what his perfect girl looks like, but he never believed in finding her. He never imagined spending time with her, holding her hand, or taking her on dates.

Belief isn't everything, however. For many years, I was swayed by the power of belief, which was the reason why I didn't accomplish much until I realized this. I thought that if you believe it, it will come true. If you believe in yourself, you can do the extraordinary. The primary function of belief is to counter doubt, to help you form strong intentions.

Step One, the Intention, has everything to do with the brain, mind, cognition, belief, thought, and imagination. Treat your intention separately as its own little world. It is the first component of a three-part system. It is the ultimate starting point to changing your energy.

Step 2 — Attention

Attention, on the other hand, has everything to do with focus and energy. It is striking how often there is a disconnect between what we want and where our focus is. Remember, what is the holdup? It is us not thinking thoughts that correspond to our desires. Even after we formed our intentions, if we continue to think about what it is and what it has always been, we will continue being out of alignment with that what we want, and as a result, be off the path of least resistance.

Where is your attention focused? Are you thinking about your bright future, or separation from it? IF you are thinking about:

- How great it **would be** to have what you want;
- How one day you **will** have it;
- How you **will** have it soon;
- How you **will** have it very soon;
- How you **want to** have it;
- How you **don't have it** right now;
- How you **haven't** obtained it yet;
- How you **never** had it;
- What it is right now;
- What it has always been.

THEN you are acknowledging the fact that you don't have it **right now**. In that moment, your attention is on separation from your desired future. Where your attention goes, your energy flows. You are saying, I want this, but right now I am here, and therefore I don't have it. Your attention continues to feed what it is and what it has always been with energy, expanding it. As a result, you continue to attract just that, the lack of that what you want.

We have to ignore the absence of what we don't have or the presence of what we don't want to have. The only thoughts we should be entertaining is the pleasure deriving from already having that what we desire.

You must unite with your future in your present moment. That is how you will accelerate the process of absorbing it into your three-dimensional reality.

Take your flashcard, place it about two feet in front of you with the letter facing up. Imagine that there is a path that goes from you to the flashcard. A straight, wonderful, amazing, magnificent path that takes you right to your desired future. Whenever you focus on what it is and what it has always been, you step off of that path, because your thoughts no longer correspond with your desires.

Your intention must be aligned with your attention.

To stay on the path, you have to think about that what you want as if it has already happened, otherwise you are out of alignment. Specifically, you have to be vibrating on the same frequency as the quantum possibility of the goal you wish to achieve. You must be a vibrational match to that possibility.

Some examples:

- Instead of I'm tired of being broke, say I'm wealthy;
- Instead of I want to find love, say I found love;
- Instead of I can't get healthy, say I'm healthy;
- Instead of I was never successful, say I'm successful;
- Instead of I am a future author, say I'm an author.

Otherwise, you will always be a future author, you will always want to find love, and you will continue never being successful. Do you see this? When you say I'm tired of being broke, where does your attention go? The golden rule is: **do not put anything into your consciousness that you do not want to manifest**.

In no city, country, continent, altitude, nowhere in this universe, can you focus your thoughts on what you do not want and end up with what you do want. You still have to put in the work, which is why on the back of your flashcards you wrote your actionable steps.

Working hard but acknowledging the lack of that what you want is like stepping on the gas and the brake at the same time. It wears down the brakes, and puts a lot of strain on the engine, while wasting a lot of fuel. It's not efficient. Remember, the universe responds to the thoughts you keep thinking.

Trying to execute all of the steps on the back of your card, but placing your attention on the separation from that which you are trying to accomplish wastes a lot of energy. I'm not saying you won't get there, but it will be much harder.

What will the thoughts of how you have no money, how you will never afford things you want, and how much you hate your life because of all that do?

Moreover, how would you feel, acknowledging those things? Motivated, driven, and energized to accomplish your amazing new future? Probably not, because those thoughts of separation carry some heavy feelings. Then why do it?

What is interesting, is that it is a cycle. The more you place your attention on being broke, the worse you feel. The worse you feel, the more financial instability you attract. The more financial instability you attract, the worse you feel, and that attracts more financial instability. How do we break the cycle? By shifting our attention to that which we want, rather than what it has always been.

I can explain this to you in any way you want. Physically, you become less motivated and enthusiastic. Energetically, you are feeding the bad with your attention, and thus your energy flows to that which you don't want, expanding it. Quantum physically, you are not aligning yourself with your ideal future.

Do you see why some people inadvertently use the law of attraction to their detriment? They attract what they do not want, by placing their attention on exactly that. Do not place your attention on anything you do not want to manifest, unless it is for damage control purposes. Align your intention with your attention. We can't go without this if we want to change our energy and our life.

Step 3 — Feeling

This is where the bar that separates the 1% from 99% of people is. We can form clear intentions and have our attention laser-focused on them, but without a corresponding feeling, those intentions remain to be just words on a flashcard.

Where I went wrong myself for many years was that I thought that thoughts create reality, and so we had to think wisely. I felt like I was on the right track, casting all doubt and not putting anything into my consciousness that I didn't want to manifest. Yet I was missing the third most important element. My thoughts without feeling continued to be simply images of imagination.

Our goal is simple, it is to *connect* to the unified field of energy that contains our quantum potentials, *see* the potentials, *tune into them* with our feelings, and *absorb* them into our three-dimensional reality. Connect, see, tune it, absorb. We can imagine the field of energy and connect to it; we can imagine our future and see it; but without feeling, we cannot tune into it to absorb it. A disconnect will remain.

There are portions of the Bible that have been purposefully taken out for some reason. One of those texts was the *Gospel of Thomas.* It contains the actual words of Jesus when he spoke teaching the power of emotion in healing others. In verse forty-eight, it says when you make thought and emotion one, "they will say to the mountain 'Move Away,' and it will move away."[22] You may not be able to move a mountain, but nonetheless, thought and feeling have to make peace. They must agree with each other and come together in the heart, because the unified field of energy that holds all of the electromagnetic potentials only understands what is in the heart.

The field does not understand vision boards, or words, or thoughts. It understands energy, because it is energy. The father of quantum theory, Max Planck, said that there is a field of energy that holds everything together.[23] In the 1800s, a similar belief evolved, that there is a web of energy that connected everything. The field was called the "ether" field, also known as the "aether" field. [24]

In 1887, Albert A. Michelson and Edward Morley decided to test that theory, and so they conducted the Michelson-Morley experiment, but it was poorly interpreted.[25] In 1986, the experiment was repeated by the United States Air Force, with much more advanced technology, and the results were published in *Nature* magazine.

It turned out that Max Planck's theory was correct! The field was proven to exist. This was absolutely astonishing because the field is completely invisible yet present all around us. Moreover, it measured precisely as Michelson and Morley predicted, a hundred years earlier. Furthermore, the physical composition of the field was identified. The studies showed that it is made out of electrical and magnetic energy, emitting electromagnetic waves.[26]

Why is this a big deal? We have two organs in our body that emit electromagnetic waves. One is our brain, and another is our heart. Yet our

---

[22] Lambdin (trans.), *Gospel of Thomas*, verse 48, p. 6.

[23] Stuewer, "Max Planck," Britannica.

[24] Wikipedia, "Aether theories."

[25] Wikipedia, "Michelson-Morley experiment."

[26] Silvertooth, "Special Relativity," Nature, p. 590.

heart is 5000 times electromagnetically more powerful than our brain. [27] And all feelings come from where? The heart.

When we place our attention on our intention and send it through the heart, it translates the image of our imagination into an electromagnetic message that the ether field can now read. Thus, **experiencing feelings that you imagine your future would bring you is how the unified field of electromagnetic potentials will understand you**. That is why we have to imagine how it would feel to have that what we want as if it already happened.

When thinking about this consider the following:

- How joyful it feels;
- How satisfied you feel to have it;
- How happy you feel;
- How relieved you feel;
- How much love you feel;
- Feeling in awe;
- Being in love with life;
- Worthy;
- How relaxed you feel;
- How content you feel;
- How GRATEFUL you feel for already having it.

These emotions are the energy that will carry your intent.

If we want to heal another person, we have to imagine that person already being healed, believe in them being healed, and experience the feeling of them being healed.

You can repeat the affirmation, I am rich, I am healthy, I am successful, until you are blue in the face, but if it is the feeling of being poor, in pain, and unsuccessful is all you feel, the thought of being rich, healed and successful will never make it past your brainstem. You are stuck in Step One. **You can think positively all you want, but without the corresponding**

---

[27] Amorim, "The heart is 5000 times stronger magnetically than the brain!"

feeling or emotion equal to that thought, your message cannot be understood by the quantum field, and you cannot attract that what you desire.

So, if you live in fear or lack, but think about abundancy, you cannot create abundancy, because change can only happen when your thoughts are in alignment with your emotions. That is what changes your energy, and that is what generates the quantum event. Meanwhile, **a series of quantum events is what changes your life.** Hence, when you change your energy, you will change your life.

The Quantum Event occurs when you marry your thoughts (intention) and your feelings. THAT causes infinite fields of energy to collapse into particles that become matter, and matter takes shape of people, events, and circumstances around the world that all begin to align to manifest into your three-dimensional world. That occurrence is called a *quantum event*. Whenever there is a match between your energy and the energy of your *future quantum possibility*, it will find you!

A common problem is that people are stuck in a loop where thoughts of what they don't want to keep attracting just that, and reinforcing their lack of belief in that which they do want. Just like in the example above about money.

Many people try to move away from their problems, and for a few months they feel better; but then, somehow, those past problems begin to find them. You can change a relationship, or a job, or a place of living all you want, but UNLESS you change your magnetism (your energy), you will continue attracting the old issues in a new relationship, at your new job, or in your new place.

There is another component to this. At times, you may imagine the feeling of solving a particular problem, but you may not fully believe in its solution. So, no matter how much you say, "I solved the problem," if you do not believe in that, a disconnect will remain between the heart and the brain. In Kinesiology, it is even measured by electrical impulse shortages, when our thoughts do not agree with our feelings.

When this happens, our message to the field, although still communicated, is very weak. This is where the power of belief gets mixed into the power of our feelings. Believing in something is not what communicates it to the field. As you remember, belief is in Step One along with thoughts and imagination. It is a cognitive component, not an emotional one. Yet lack of belief weakens the feelings we can experience, in association with the possibility we are trying to manifest. This is why we must cast out all doubt.

Remember, a strong *brain-heart* connection creates a strong *heart-field* connection. Believe what you feel, believe what you imagine. In the quantum of possibilities, anything is possible. Except for you growing a pair of wings and flying away.

Finally, the four big mistakes that many people make when trying to align their intention, attention, and feeling.

1) Never put a time frame on when you will expect it to happen. It is unknown.

Let's say you set out to make $800,000 by the age of thirty. As you turn twenty-nine and a half, and look at your bank account, noticing a considerable lack of any sum that is even remotely close to $800,000, what will you think about? If you are like most people, you will probably think about how you are still far away from that amount. Where does your attention go then? On the separation from that what you want, and so your Step Two is now missing. In that moment, your attention is no longer aligned with your intention and feeling.

Live knowing, is knowing that it will all happen in its divine time. You don't know when, nobody knows, only divine intelligence possesses that knowledge.

2) Don't try to predict how it will happen. It is unknown.

There is a hidden danger in this. I remember when I first decided to test out this practice, I tried to manifest $5,000. At that time, I had just started working as a lawyer. In our law firm, at the end of the month, we were given bonuses for the cases we settled. I decided I wanted to make $5,000 in bonuses.

So, I imagined how it would feel to walk into my boss' office, how he would tell me the good news, and how absolutely ecstatic I would feel in the moment. As the month progressed, I saw that the money from the cases I settled wasn't going to be coming in this month. This made me realize the sad, unfortunate truth — that a $5,000 bonus will continue to be just a dream. In that moment, I felt the awful separation. I returned back to feeling the same old familiar emotions that acknowledged the lack of that what I wanted.

The next month, I set out to meet the same goal, but this time I imagined just the $5,000. It didn't matter where it came from. In the next four days, I received a notice from a retirement fund that I had completely forgotten I created when I was working for the city as an Administrative Hearing Officer three years before. The letter notified me that the amount I had accrued was $5,041. I stood speechless in the middle of my room for a few seconds, which was immediately followed by an outburst of laughter and joyfulness.

We don't know how that what we want will happen, so avoid placing any particularity on your dreams. Imagine the end result, and accept that the journey will always surprise you.

3) Don't be attached to a particular outcome, it may come to you in a very different form than you expect.

This one is tricky. If you experience an outcome that is different from that what you tried to achieve, don't label it as good or bad, successful or not successful, right or wrong. It will seem bad in the moment, or simply different from that what you tried to achieve, but end up taking you exactly where you wanted to be.

For example, when I came back from Russia, I wanted to manifest finding a job as a paralegal at a firm that would later hire me as a lawyer. I found a job at a prestigious law firm in Brentwood. I was so grateful and endlessly thankful to the Universe for giving me this opportunity. Everything was perfect. Yet, just two weeks later, I got laid off.

I thought to myself, "This is horrible, this is awful, how could this be? This was that job I dreamed of, and now I lost it." However, the next day, I centered myself and realigned my intention, attention, and feeling.

Four days later, I reconnected with my old law school friend, Manny. He ended up hiring me as his paralegal, paid me for two months of Bar prep, helped me pass the Bar, and hired me as an attorney. We have been working together ever since. He later became my client for my consulting business. By working with him, I was able to create a fully automated law consultant program that skyrocketed our firm's profits. I ended up making a killing on transforming other lawyers' law firms and their lives using this program.

You see, me getting fired was a blessing in disguise, yet in the moment, it seemed like a complete failure. We just don't know. So, no matter what happens, don't label it as good or bad, because if you label it as bad, your attention will once again be on the lack, or separation from that what you want, and your Step Two will be missing.

4) Never shift back into thinking thoughts that do not correspond with what you want.

This also trips up a lot of people, because, don't forget, everything will happen in its divine time. You don't know when. So many people who don't see immediate results, give up and shift back into their old ways of thinking.

Then they definitely don't achieve that what they want, because their attention and feeling are missing. As a result, they continue to see their past re-created in their present and future, thinking that this whole strategy doesn't work. This creates doubt and takes them even further away from manifesting their desires.

Stay consistent, my friend. Some things may take five minutes to manifest, some five months, some five years. It will happen when it is supposed to happen, as long as you *allow* it to. The reason why people don't get to where they want, is because of this very mistake. They lose focus and resort back into operating from a doubting mentality, rather than a knowing mentality. Doubt destroys intention, attention, and feeling. Allow the future you want to come to you. Stay aligned.

As a final and very short exercise to finish off this chapter, I invite you to look in the mirror and let it reflect exactly the person that you want it to reflect. Do this every day; even thirty seconds is enough. However, really experience the feeling of being the person you wish to be. Look at yourself, and consciously go over every feeling associated with being that individual. This is how you bring the extraordinary results into your life with ease, and become limitless.

Chapter 17

Limitless Happiness

What if we could be limitlessly happy? Boy, wouldn't that be nice? That would mean that our happiness would never end! Well, I have news for you, my friend: that is already the case, because our true happiness comes from within us. Happiness is an innate part of us, it is inherent. Being happy is actually our natural state of being, and is part of our DNA. So, in a way, as long as we live, we have the ability to always be limitlessly happy.

You may ask, well, how come so many people are unhappy then? There are hundreds of reasons. Leo Tolstoy, a famous Russian writer, once said, "We all have different ways to be happy, but we all have the same ways to be miserable."

There is countless wisdom in those words. To some happiness is family, to others it is creating art, for me it is making a difference in my environment. However, to all, a loss of something meaningful, seeing a loved one pass, or getting injured brings them misery and suffering.

So, this chapter is not going to be about what to do to be happy, as much as what to do to avoid unhappiness. Our happiness can be fragile. Yet notice I say, *can be*. It doesn't have to be, if you are equipped with two things. One, tools to deal with suffering; and two, the ability to not sabotage your happiness. Once we have those two in place, I will tell you the formula for happiness.

Happiness is double-sided. On one side, there are things we can do to promote it, and on another, things we can avoid to not sabotage it. It is a craft, and we can master it.

Dealing with Suffering

You are already years ahead of most people because you have already learned how to deal with stress, fear, anger, and doubt. Those four can powerfully decrease one's happiness. This is why we focus so much on the power of calmness and trusting the Universe. However, all of those brilliant tactics in this book and many other books sometimes don't work. Why? Because we are human.

It is not about getting a perfect score, but having the tools to get a perfect score.

The biggest variable that remains is life. Life happens, unexpected events occur, and we have no control for the most part.

I wrote this book, and I still experience some stress, fear, doubt, and anger. Significantly less than I did when I was twenty-five, but our human experience goes on, and continues to test us. Part of being happy is being able to accept that. The more we battle and disagree with the events that make us experience negative emotions, the more we prolong our suffering.

Recently, I sold a stock right before it went up. In five days, I could have made $68,000. I regretted that decision. I felt stupid, left out, angry, stressed, and of course that day I wasn't very happy. Actually, I wasn't feeling happy at all. If anything, I was on a completely polar opposite side of the spectrum of happiness.

Welcoming it with calmness didn't help; thinking that the Universe is perfect didn't help; thinking that this may actually be a good thing in the long run, but my awareness is limited, and my knowledge is incomplete, and only the divine intelligence knows what good will come out of this, didn't help.

I felt powerless. So, I sat and processed my feelings. I acknowledged it. I asked myself how do I feel? Why do I feel this way? Why is this bothering me so much? This was a pivotal moment that tested my theory about happiness. Overall, I was still happy, but in that moment, I didn't feel like it at all.

My friend, that is okay. What is not okay, is suppressing those emotions. When something unfavorable happens, two things can occur. We can either respond to it with calmness and not create an array of negative emotions, or we can react emotionally. However, if we take the second option, we have to allow ourselves to feel those emotions, to deal with them, to process them, to welcome them.

If we suppress them by shifting our attention to something else, just so that we could avoid feeling them, they will rot inside of us. It's like somebody dumping toxins onto your beautiful backyard, and instead of taking the time to neutralize them, you get an excavator and effortlessly dig a huge hole to throw all of the toxins in there, and cover it with green grass. Then you won't have to get your hands dirty, and just continue enjoying your beautiful backyard. Yet, with time the toxins will spread, and the land will be poisoned, and all the plants that grow on your backyard will die. That is what happens to us if we don't resolve the negative emotions that we feel as a result of dealing with life's surprises.

Part of being happy is being able to accept. The more we fight the events that make us experience stress, fear, regret, and doubt, the more we suffer. I could have spent days, months, or years, regretting my stock trading decision. Nothing would change, except I would feel extremely unhappy for much longer.

However, trusting the Universe, not judging circumstances as good or bad, and responding with calmness, are muscles that we can strengthen. The more we try to respond with calmness, the better we will get at it.

Responding with calmness should be our ultimate goal, because if we do that, the less negative emotions we will create that we then would have to process and deal with later. Moreover, the less misfortune we would attract because our emotions are energy and we attract with our energy, as we learned earlier.

There are some things that we may never be able to respond with calmness to, or judge as not good or bad, and that is okay. Just like no matter how much we train, there are some exercises that we may never be able to do, but we could do many others. The stronger our ability to not be negatively impacted by our human experience becomes, the less suffering we will experience.

How to Not Sabotage Our Happiness

The second part that will help us avoid unhappiness is recognizing that we have been conditioned to be unhappy. Many people experience this idea that "If I get something, then I will be happy." This could be anything, a house, a girlfriend, a new job, or a meditation technique. What happens to your happiness if you don't get it then? Or if you get it, but then you lose it? That is where the pitfall lies that we have to be aware of.

My friend, I invite you to realize that **there is nothing you can get to make you happy,** because true happiness comes from within. Just accept that **nothing and no one will ever make you happy.** There are things that you can get that will make you feel satisfied, excited, or accomplished, but not happy. Those feelings fade. No one is as excited about their new car a year later as they were on the day when they got it.

Eckhart Tolle once said, "There are two ways of being unhappy; one is not getting what you want, and another is getting what you want."

Attaching an idea of happiness to anything we can lose, is setting ourselves up for a very unhappy result. Why do that? Why condition ourselves to be unhappy? The minute we stop relying on something to make us happy is the minute that we free our happiness. Moreover, our brain is biologically wired to respond more to the anticipation of the reward, rather than the reward itself. So then, thinking that getting something will make you happy really becomes meaningless.

Happiness is in the Journey

For many years, I myself fell into the trap of thinking that if I get something, then I will be happy. I visualized everyday things that I thought would make me happy. I thought about taking a vacation, being done with exams, or getting my dream car.

The day before every vacation, I felt ecstatic. The whole week was ahead, and I could not stop thinking about all the things I would do and see. That anticipation brought me so much joy. However, once I finally got to the place, it felt good, but I did not feel as excited as I was right before. The magic was sort of gone.

When I studied for my exams, I dreamed of the day when this misery would be over. I envisioned the amazing freedom of not having to study, and finally having my life back. Nevertheless, once I walked out of that test center, and the future I had waited for so long finally became the present, I actually felt empty, with this strange sensation of meaninglessness hovering beneath me.

I remembered the great satisfaction I derived from looking at pictures of my dream car and imagining having it, driving it and showing it. I thought, the day I get it will be life-altering. Though when I finally got the keys handed to me, it did not feel as spectacular, instead it felt kind of usual and normal.

It always felt like the future seemed brighter until it became the present, and I just could never understand why. Yet, one day I set out to solve this mystery, and take control of my happiness.

The answer lay in the United States' *Declaration of Independence*. The Founding Fathers believed that the "unalienable rights" were "Life, Liberty and the pursuit of Happiness." There is so much wisdom in these words because it is indeed a "pursuit" and not achievement of happiness.

Several studies have measured blood flow and oxygenation levels both in anticipation of the reward and actually taking possession of it. The results demonstrated that the endorphin receptors of the brain fired more in anticipation of the reward, rather than when getting the reward itself.[28] This is because our brain is biologically wired to respond more to the thrill of seeking. We were designed this way on purpose because that is what helped us survive since the beginning of humankind.[29]

---

[28] Zweig, "Your money and your brain"; and Willis, and Haines, "The Limbic System."
[29] ScienceBlog, "Happiness: A Theory — Jaak Panksepp And The Seeking System."

Imagine if it was the other way around. If we derived more pleasure from the end result, then we would only go for things that were readily available, and never accomplish anything. We would not even be here right now, because our ancestors would have never hunted, conquered land, or built social unions that developed into societies.

All of that is the process. Because of the anticipation circuitry in our brain, having things just given to us in life, no matter how valuable they may be, does not feel as good as anticipating them. This is why, when our needs are passively met, we feel bored, because we diminish our own happiness.[30]

We have all seen people who just have things handed to them. They may have it all, but their eyes gloom with indifference, and their heart is punctured with a hole that has to be filled with bodily pleasures. It's not that they don't appreciate what they have because they never had to work for it, but because they never got a chance to experience the happiness of the anticipation of the reward; they were just given it. So, they skipped out on the whole amazing, spectacular dopamine journey.

For years, I have asked myself, "How could this be? If I had everything they have, I would be forever happy." I did not realize how our brain was designed back then. It was never about what one has, but the process of attaining it. That's the stimulating part.

No matter how incredibly amazing we may feel when we finally acquire everything we ever wanted, the good feeling of having it will always fade. This is why. "There are two ways of being unhappy; one is not getting what you want, and another is getting what you want."

Happiness is in the movement. Happiness is the journey, it is growth, a constant change. It is in our continuous progress, where we feel alert, alive, and interested. This stimulates our curiosity to see what the world will bring us tomorrow, and what discoveries we will make in ourselves today. Yet with no movement, there is no anticipation, no seeking and no pursuit.

Sometimes we may not get to where we wanted to be, and that is okay. Remember, it is not about the end result, and there is nothing you can get to be happy. This is why I invite you to enjoy every process and every journey that you undertake in pursuit of your goals.

---

[30] Loehr, The Only Way to Win, p. 4

Some may understand the word "achievement" as the end result. So, promoting achievement may seem contradictory, because our brain is biologically wired to respond more to the thrill of seeking rather than the attainment of the end result.

Yes, we do feel happier in the anticipation of the reward, but every achievement is simply part of the process. Every accomplishment takes us further in life. If we constantly set goals and try to accomplish them, we will always be in the movement, always anticipating, always moving, and thus always having the ability to feel excited and alive.

Some may ask, but what about our success? If we constantly work on something and derive great happiness from the process, but don't get anywhere, then what's the point? Don't trouble yourself with this. You will get somewhere eventually, and if you don't, then at the very least you would live an exciting and enjoyable life. That's the point, that is success.

I know plenty of people who accomplished tremendously remarkable achievements but were miserable in the process, and then they died feeling like life was too short. The worst part is that because of the anticipatory circuitry of our brain, they couldn't enjoy the end result that much, and at the same time, they couldn't go back in time and relive the journey to enjoy it more. Now, that is a shitty situation to be in, not having few accomplishments on your resume.

Goals are like a mirage: once we get there, we see that there is nothing there, and so we are off to the next one. Just like with our vacations, getting a new car, or finally being done with exams. Once we are there, we realize it was all a mirage, and so we are off to planning something new and looking forward to something else. When we finally recognize that **goals are set to create direction in life**, we no longer have to worry about sabotaging our happiness as a result of not attaining that what we set out to get.

How to Promote More Happiness

As promised, once we have the two components in place that will help avoid unhappiness, I would share with you the formula to promote happiness. Aristotle once said, "To be happy, dedicate yourself to the development of your natural talents and abilities by doing what you love to do and invest into doing it better and better in the service of a cause that is greater than yourself." As you can see, a big component of this is movement. Setting goals and striving to accomplish them in the area that aligns with our natural talents and abilities.

Also, if one follows this, think about how much self-advancement that person will experience in the process. I believe we live when we evolve, that is what makes life interesting, and that definitely contributes to our happiness. It is true that "greatness finds learners" as Robin Sharma said. Under this model, not only we would be achieving personal goals, but we would also be working toward a goal greater than us. That would give us a feeling of purpose.

Those who think highly of themselves for accumulating wealth will die unremembered and unsatisfied. People remember us for how we made them feel, not what we had. Nobody at any person's funeral will remember them for how many cars they had, how big their pool was, or how many acres they owned.

People will remember how that person made them feel; they will remember them for the impact they had on their life; how that person was there for them during tough times; for the contributions they made to the society, that live long after they are gone; the positive change they promoted; the art, literature, or any material they publicized that continues to influence people in this world.

So, Aristotle's idea truly does appear to be a very effective formula for happiness. Doing what we love so that we are eager to learn more about it for the benefit of a cause greater than ourselves.

Of course, not all of us like doing something that will better the world. However, don't exclude a possibility that you may either just not know what that is yet, or underestimate the impact of that what you are doing already.

You have no idea the lengths I had to go through to find a good mechanic. It was nearly impossible. Every single one I encountered or was recommended, either had no idea what they were doing or charged too much.

When I finally found one (and that was after I realized how to use the law of attraction to my advantage), I felt blessed. Many may say, "But he's just a mechanic." I disagree, I think a good mechanic is God-sent to this earth. Just think about how much good he has done for people. How much time and money he saved them; how he brought those cars that may be so meaningful to their owners back to life; how many legendary vehicles he returned to the roads to continue carrying out their legacy.

You see, a sense of purpose can be tied to most professions or businesses. I appreciate and love the janitor at our law office building so much. Every day, I get to come to a clean office where the trash is taken out, everything smells good, and the tables are disinfected. I get to wash my hands in a sink where the faucet is flawlessly clean and shining. When I fix my tie in the mirror, the mirror is perfectly spotless. Maybe to him, it is just a job, but he makes such a big difference in my day. No matter what you do, I believe there is a way to derive meaning from it, unless the one and only person that is benefited by your craft is you.

As to the other point that Aristotle makes, yes, it would be fantastic to do what we love and invest into doing it better, but only if it is lucrative, and is not detrimental to us. Some people love smoking weed, yet investing into doing it better is not going to make them very happy in the long run. Others absolutely love playing games on their phone, they are thrilled by it, but it's a bit hard to make a living out of that.

A gap that some of us may fall into pursuing Aristotle's formula, is spending too much time devising this perfect combination of doing what we love that makes money and a difference in the lives of others, consequently delaying the start of their journey indefinitely. As a result, we may not get very far with our happiness or in life. I think there is a simpler approach.

Meaningful Life

I believe that as long as we serve a cause that is greater than ourselves, we will always live with meaning. Living for something greater than us takes a lot of attention off of ourselves, and so we become less concerned about personal dissatisfactions that can sabotage our happiness.

When all of our attention is on us, we are walking on thin ice. Think about it, if our world revolves around us and something happens to us or our immediate possessions, the whole world comes crashing down. That consumes a lot of energy, and leaves us worried about meaningless things that are only meaningful to us. What does this do to our happiness?

If our vision is broader, and we take up a small part of a large world that we serve and something happens to us, the world still stands. Imagine if your mission in life is to lead a spiritual awakening, and you get your car stolen. That would matter a lot less to you than to someone who lives for themselves, because your attention is on something so much bigger than your earthly possessions. You don't have to be Elon Musk or the Dalai Lama. **Your vision of serving a cause greater than yourself lies in your perspective.** Consider my examples about the mechanic and the janitor. They can attach great meaning to their jobs, by simply changing how they perceive them.

I noticed that people who don't have a broader vision are always looking for motivation. A big part of a reason for that is because they constantly battle their ego in trying to motivate themselves to get things done. Inspiration is something more powerful than our ego and all of its illusions. If we are inspired by a cause greater than ourselves, an invisible force takes us by the hand and leads us to where the Universe needs us to be. That inspiration can come from your perspective of that which you do. Contrary to that, even Elon Musk can look at everything he has done as meaningless, because nothing lasts forever, everything has an end.

What is the difference between having a goal and having a purpose? A goal is something we accomplish, a purpose is something we continuously pursue, just like happiness. There is no end. Such an ongoing expectancy goes back to the anticipation circuitry in our brain. We can forever improve something, and see the difference it makes for those around us. Do you see how limitless this can be?

Why did Aristotle stress the importance of "Dedicating yourself to the development of your natural talents and abilities by doing what you love to do and investing into doing it better and better?" Because a large portion of happiness is in the movement.

Remember the story about Jeffrey from the box and Henry the millionaire? What happened to them? What destroyed their mind, body, and spirit, and made their happiness follow the crumbling downward path? It was lack of movement. The section of that chapter, "A slow death," is not just about our power of will going stale, it is also about diminishing our happiness.

I get it, to each, happiness is different. However, I can't say I agree with Leo Tolstoy fully. Perhaps happiness is different to each in the moment, but what about long term? To one, getting wasted makes them very happy, but then health problems begin to catch up that diminish their enjoyment of anything. Will that person be happy in the end?

To another, writing endlessly, ignoring all other aspects of their life, is happiness, because that is what they love to do, especially if they feel like their writing is making an impact on a cause greater than themselves, which gives them a great sense of purpose and meaning. But what about friends, being loved, feeling of belongingness, having someone to care for them and care for? All of that will inevitably leave a hole in their heart that will have to be filled with something. Will they be happy, years down the line?

To someone else, happiness is being healthy and having a fit body that is capable of the extraordinary, however, if they don't have money to satisfy their natural needs, they will suffer.

I know plenty of very spiritually successful people who achieve astral projection, out-of-body experiences, and feel the most unearthly sensations when they cultivate their consciousness and their energy body. Unfortunately, when they return to the physical world, they experience real-life problems that occur because they have not mastered the material human experience, which all takes a toll on their well-being and makes them want to escape into the realms of endless exploration of the unified field of energy.

I believe long-term happiness is the same for all of us because it lies in tapping into our natural, innate state of being.

I personally have mastered Aristotle's formula in several areas of my life. I love being a life coach and a consultant because I feel like I'm positively influencing the world, one person at a time; I love being an employment lawyer defending employees' rights and reshaping businesses in the state of California for the better; I love working out and helping others get in better shape; I love writing and giving people the knowledge to master their lives; I love creating virtual reality galleries and augmented reality projector art shows with underlying spiritual messages, because I feel like it expands people's imaginations and shows them how possible it is to live extraordinary lives. Yet with all of that, I still wasn't happy.

Why? You would think I would be the happiest person alive, or at least Aristotle would think so.

Before my trip to Mexico in December 2020, I couldn't stop doing, designing, devising, drawing, creating, building, customizing, writing, doing group meditations, working out, improving my memory, my speaking skills, my social media presence, creating content, learning new law, tai-chi, new meditation techniques, filming, traveling, and the list goes on. All of that was, of course, stimulated by enormous amounts of caffeine and sugar. I just could not stop.

I was addicted to this dopamine rush of anticipating the result of that which I was excited to achieve. I was in love with the process, and I could not bear the idea of just being present with myself, going for a hike that didn't involve some exhilarating climb, swimming in a pool, or just doing nothing. I reasoned, "Why would I do all that boring shit? My lifestyle is amazing, I am happy."

If anything, I wanted to escape the feeling of being bored as much as possible, and replace it with an endless chase for stimulation. I was on a crash course, without even knowing. My addiction to dopamine and my inability to just be were big indicators, but I ignored them.

I ignored those indicators, just as I ignored the majority of my unpleasant emotions. Those emotions came from childhood, teen years, and even some more recent events. They were anger, a feeling of being judged, rejection, annoyance, and many others.

The more emotions I repressed by staying busy, the less I had to deal with. I just didn't want to feel them. However, all of those unresolved feelings began to show up in my inability to enjoy my natural, innate state of happiness.

In my natural state, I wasn't happy. Instead, I was negative, judgmental, and angry, because the second I slowed down and allowed myself to just be, all this shit I repressed would come up, and I would be far from happy.

Instead of processing my unpleasant emotions, I numbed them with a giant wave of pleasant ones. I used my lifestyle to suppress those emotions, and it worked brilliantly, but I was getting close to the expiration date.

I noticed that my projects didn't give me as much excitement anymore. So, I had to pursue bigger ones, feel more stimulation, drink stronger coffee. This went on for three months, until I could not be present at all. Every second I spent awake, my mind was racing, analyzing, concluding, proving these conclusions wrong with new ones. I felt like I was bouncing on the walls of my own mind, and didn't know how to stop it. All I knew is that I was getting very exhausted. I began having days when I was so energetically depleted by the end, that I couldn't talk, think, or see anyone. The only thing I was capable of was closing my eyes, and dipping into the darkness behind my eyelids.

A trip to Mexico is what saved me.

Letting Go

I was visiting my girlfriend Delia in Cancun. While there, we ended up going to this shamanic village in the jungle, called Portal Xibalba. The atmosphere there was mesmerizing. I felt like we were in some lost, alien civilization. They had buildings four stories high, made out of rocks and trees; they had temples built in a shape of a human head with eyes and ears; there were breathtaking caves with freshwater underneath the ground; everything and everyone was part of nature and completely off the grid.

We got there at nine in the morning, and stayed until the next day. It was the very first time in the last ten years that I sat doing nothing for ten hours. No phone, no internet, no VR goggles, no augmented reality projector to create on, no paper to draw on, nothing to read, nothing to write with, we were just one on one with nature and ourselves.

I felt bored. Even worse, I was forced to be just one on one with myself. I began to feel negative, judgmental, and uneasy. Little did I know, I was in the midst of my spiritual awakening. It felt fucking horrible. I was left no choice but to connect with my true self, and see all the shit that was hiding inside of me, suppressed deep down in the core of my subconscious.

That was when I began to awake to remembrance of who I truly was. I caught myself being extremely present, and I could not recall when the last time was that I felt this way. I began to notice how I felt. Emotions like pain, abandonment, anger, anxiety, disappointment, sadness, indifference, lack of motivation, depression, all began to come up. It was unlike anything I was ever used to. It was so painful and uncomfortable.

I felt like I was being ripped apart by the low vibrational frequencies of those emotions. It was so far away from happiness and how I was used to feeling in my everyday life. I didn't feel like myself. Yet I knew that this was the time that I had to finally deal with everything I had repressed for years. I had to. If not now, then when, I asked? Later? Well, later is now.

I fought these painful feelings for about six hours. At one point, I got so tired of resisting that I just said, "Fine, take me." I sat there and let all of those emotions just be. I absorbed and felt every single one to the fullest. I was scared.

Yet, one by one, I acknowledged every emotion, accepted it, gave it compassion, and released it into the light. I pictured the light to be this healing power that welcomed everything I gave it. That was when I began transcending through my emotions. This went on for about two hours, and it was only the beginning.

The second component was to go back to all past experiences, and process those emotions. I went as far back as I could remember. I began in order from years predating kindergarten, all the way to my most recent experiences. Every time I felt something, I acknowledged it, accepted it, gave it compassion, and released it into the light. This was a lengthy and agonizing process. I wanted to quit at least twenty times, I just wanted to pull the plug and go back to my perfect life, but I knew that if not now, then never.

With every emotion I peeled off, I felt lighter and more relieved. However, this didn't work for all of them. Some emotions were stuck so deep, that no matter how much I tried to acknowledge them, they would remain stuck inside of me. I felt the build-up. It was a heavy feeling in my chest that began to rise up into my throat. It felt like there was a clot in my esophagus, making it harder to breathe. I felt like I wanted to just release.

I exited the temple and ran into the jungle. The build-up was getting more and more intense, it was growing into nausea. I ran faster, but that didn't help. I flexed my whole body, that didn't help; I clenched my jaw, I dug my nails into my palms, I squeezed a tree as hard as I could, but none of that helped.

Finally, I stopped. I leaned back while standing arching my spine, looked into the sky, and fucking screamed as loud as I could. I thought about all of the emotions that I wanted to release, and so I screamed louder and longer. It was an amazing feeling. It was like an energetic vomit, where all the shit that was rotting inside of me finally exploded out of me. This went on for about ten minutes. I would stop when I would feel like it was over, sense the heavy pressuring sensation building up, and I would scream again.

After my last outburst, I collapsed on the debris beneath me. Both of my palms were flat on the ground. I felt the earth. I felt its grounding, massive, blissful energy. Everything stopped. I was breathing very heavily. In that moment, I noticed something I didn't expect. It was a feeling of weightlessness. I had never had such a sensation of lightness and calmness combined together before.

I felt an extreme relief, the nausea was gone, the pressure from my chest dissipated, my throat felt like it expanded, and I could breathe with ease. I walked back to Portal Xibalba confused as to what just happened. All I knew was that those emotions were released. I felt free.

When I came back into the temple, I was tremendously surprised at how quickly this comforting, warm feeling of lightness began to rise up. I felt more present. The only thing is that my voice was gone.

At that time, I thought I was done, but boy, I was wrong. Life continues to happen, memories continue to come up, and we have to continue dealing with feelings and emotions. And that is okay. **However, if we don't deal with them, and we don't release them, it will be very hard for our happiness to come from within, because within us would be all this darkness, overshadowing our innate state of happiness.**

If we accept whatever we feel as just a feeling, it will be easier to let go. Our ego labels everything because it is the voice of duality. Our ego tells us that this feeling is good or bad. We instinctively want to fight everything that is bad.

If we see it as just being, we don't have to fight it anymore or disagree with it. It becomes much easier to just feel it and process it, instead of rejecting it and suppressing it. This may seem painful at first, and you may feel actually less happy, because you are now acknowledging what doesn't feel so good. Yet in the long run, this is where long-term happiness lies.

It is a process. Our heart only sees oneness, to our heart there is no dark or light, it is all just one. Learning to look at my feelings through the eye of oneness was a great leap, and the center of my spiritual awakening. **When we bring awareness and compassion to all of our emotions, we are able to transcend through them**. I often have this imagery of rising through the emotions to a cloud of innate joy and happiness, my natural state. When I ignore my emotions, I picture the soil that I'm standing on barefoot being poisoned, and my feet are starting to burn as they sink into it.

All of our emotions are part of us, and we have to learn to love all parts of us, not just the good ones. It is easy to love yourself for being successful and excited all of the time about what tomorrow will bring. It's almost effortless. It is hard to love ourselves for all the situations we didn't handle well, and all of the shit that we have done. Without acceptance and compassion for all emotions, we are rejecting part of ourselves, and that rejection will always impact our natural state of happiness.

We can plant the green grass on top of the poisoned land all we want, but it is just a matter of time before the toxins will come up, and we would have to shift our focus to something else. I personally thought I was chasing a good feeling that I derived from all of my activities, but no, I was escaping the bad ones inside.

After my experience in Mexico, it began to be easier to be one on one with myself, bored, sitting in a room, waiting for the elevator, going on a hike, or staring at traffic. Also, many things began to bring me a lot more joy, including my meaningful life for the cause greater than me.

We cannot be light until we face the dark. What we hold back is holding us back.

Balance

After all, we can't ignore balance. Too much movement can make us ignore other areas of our life that are essential to our happiness, such as love, compassion, acknowledging our emotions, body, spirit, and sometimes, just being present.

However, if one sits in a room all day, every day, being immensely present, acknowledging all of their emotions, but not doing anything to better oneself, one will not be happy either, in my opinion.

Meanwhile, with no exercise, poor diet, and bad sleep, one can cultivate their consciousness endlessly, but when they return into their physical body, they will feel the limitations that will negatively impact their happiness.

Our life is just like the chakra system. When a person lacks a sex drive and finds themselves undesirable, their second chakra, the sacral or Svadhisthana chakra, is out of balance. However, if the person has too much sex, their sacral chakra is also out of balance. If the person cannot express themselves verbally, then their throat chakra is out of balance, but if they talk endlessly, their throat chakra is also out of balance.

I believe there has to be a balance between movement and stillness, work and pleasure, being social and going within yourself, working out and giving our body a rest.

That is why I think to master our happiness, and ultimately our life, we have to find balance not only in our daily activities, but overall, between our mind, body, and spirit.

At the same time, as long as we look for happiness elsewhere but inside of ourselves, two things will endlessly occur. We will always be dependent on that person, thing, place, substance, or whatever makes us feel good, and second, we will feel trapped, because we cannot control anything that is not within us. Meaning, the person may leave or become terminally ill, the place may become unreachable or not exist altogether, the substance may begin to affect our health, and the material thing may be taken away. What will happen to our happiness then?

So then, the question of all humanity, how do we live a happy and balanced life?

We improve ourselves in as many areas of our lives as possible to become a well-rounded person. This one sentence encapsulates everything you have read up to this point. Yet really, think about this. Dealing with our emotions is improving ourselves; dedicating ourselves to a cause greater than us is improving ourselves; improving the lives of others is improving ourselves.

These are all areas of our life because we are part of this planet and this planet is part of us. **We are all one**. Everyone and everything make a united electromagnetic field of energy. We are connected with every person, everything, everywhere, in every time. There is no just you or just me. When we understand this, selfless love overwhelms our heart with its powerful bliss, and we become limitless.

If you want your life to get better, YOU have to get better; if you want your life to change, YOU have to change. This is why all great people work on themselves more than on anything else. To have more, first, we have to be more. We cannot give if we do not have.

Striving to become a well-rounded person is an endless journey in many directions, and thus a constant discovery of self and happiness. Ultimately, success is who you are, rather than what you own. In every minute of the day lies tremendous potential. This is why time will become your biggest asset, if it hasn't already. If at the end of the day, you go to sleep a better person than you woke up, that was a great day.

The beautiful thing is that this infinite happiness is equally available to everyone. It does not matter how old you are, your background, education, or religion. True happiness is blind and it speaks all the languages. Above all, it is freedom from all the things society told us we have to have to be happy.

How in control of your happiness are you? Whether we have control over something can be easily measured. Can you improve it? If a person cannot improve their happiness, they do not have control over it. This applies to almost everything. How do we become a well-rounded person and live balanced?

To become a well-rounded person, we have to begin working on as many aspects of our life as possible. In this book, we tackle the three foundational ones, mind, body, and spirit. All other areas of our lives that we can endlessly work on stem from that. This is about becoming as resourceful as possible. Again, we cannot give, if we do not have.

Anyone can do this. Some say, I am seventy-five years old, it is too late for me to work on myself. Is it too late to be happy? Is it too late to prolong your life? Is it written somewhere, in some divine law, that once a person reaches a certain age or accomplishes a certain status, they cannot pursue happiness anymore? As long as you are alive, you can be happy. I know so many people who rose from the ashes in their worst times.

There are infinite ways to grow. The truth is, you can improve any part of you indefinitely, just like your happiness.

To summarize, here is how I see the components of a journey to limitless happiness:

1. Acknowledge your past and present emotions;
2. Serve a cause greater than yourself;
3. Do what you love and get better at it;
4. Self-advance to live balanced.

Part III

BODY

Chapter 18

Infinite Exploration of Physical Self

Why did we dedicate so many chapters to mind, and leave just one last chapter for the body? You may say, "Didn't we just talk about balance?" By no means is it less important. However, there is so much in our mind that can prevent us from ever getting to the body. For example, if we are dealing with unhappiness, inability to cope with our emotions, fear, regret, doubt, stress, and are always falling into the hoops of our mind, it will be extremely hard for us to give our body the attention it deserves.

Spirituality is always first, just like in this book. Yet, if we spend too much time cultivating our energy and ignore the body, we will throw our system out of balance, and this may affect our spiritual advancement. **The body is the spirit's temple. We must take care of the temple.**

This chapter isn't going to be long, because everyone has different physical goals, and may be in a different place with their health. This chapter will be a foundation for you to build your own house on. Physical growth is everything you do with your body. Some of the areas in this category that you can improve, but are not limited to, are exercise, diet, and sleep.

Exercise

When I was in Japan, I went to the park to work out with my Japanese friend, who I was visiting. It was a small park, with some parallel bars and a high bar. Little did I know, my entire perception of health and fitness was about to change, in the matter of one moment. By the high bar, we saw a man who looked ancient, but fit. I would guess maybe eighty-five. I instantly gave him props for just being at the park. Then I saw him reach down in his bag, and pull out what appeared to be chalk. I was puzzled. "Why would he need that?" I asked myself. He then chalked up his hands, and in one swift motion jumped on the high bar and began to hang from it.

I told my friend, "Well, that's a first." He laughed and said, "Yeah, they actually recommend older people to hang on stuff, because it's good for their spine." We were so naïve.

A few seconds passed, and this man began doing pull-ups. We started losing our minds because he was doing them so effortlessly. I personally couldn't believe it. It just didn't look right. He didn't stop at three. He did four, five, seven, ten, fifteen, and got off the bar on twenty-two. Twenty-two pull-ups!

It's hard to describe how I felt. It was a combination of confusion, disbelief, excitement, and hope. I've never seen someone this old to be this strong. I immediately asked my friend if we could come up to him.

We respectfully approached him. My friend bowed, and said, smiling, "That was a lot of pull-ups." The old man smiled back. I whispered in English, "Ask him how old he is." My friend said, "My grandfather is eighty-nine, you seem younger than him." The old man laughed, and replied, "I'm actually a little older, I am ninety-four."

I couldn't help it, I felt my eyes widening, it was almost awkward. The old man saw my reaction, and looked right at me as if he anticipated me asking the next question. I exclaimed, "How did you do twenty-two pull-ups?!" I was so emotional, that I felt like he would just miraculously understand my English. My friend translated. The man said, "Well, when I was sixty, I could do fifty pull-ups." He paused, and then in a low calm voice said the phrase that continues to echo deep down inside of me to this day. He said, "The higher you shoot the arrow into the sky, the longer it will take to come down." This happened in 2015. Since then, the most I have not worked out for was ten days.

My friend, if you are reading this when you are young, push yourself as hard as you can, for your arrow to take longer to come down. The seeds you plant today are the crops you will collect when you are older.

If you're reading this when you are around your seventies or eighties, it is not too late! You can still do much more than you think you can. Yes, it will be harder; yes, your results will be slower; and yes, it will take more discipline. Just drop all expectations and start. Just start. Start anything, it could be stretching, walking, biking, ping pong, hanging on the bar, anything. Life is movement, don't ever forget that.

As we get older, we will face three main obstacles: our body will become more fragile, our muscles will develop slower, and our desire to work out will decrease. Do not worry, there is a way to combat all of that.

My grandmother began working out at an age of seventy-seven. Before that, she had not worked out a single day in her life. On her first day, she was not able to walk up the stairs or walk more than half of a mile without a walker. Two months later, she no longer needed a walker, she could walk two miles, and walk up three flights of stairs. Every day, we did just a little more than the day before. Yet most of all, she knew, she had no doubt, that she was going to get stronger. I still remember her saying, "I just wish I did not wait this long." Cast out all doubt, my friend.

Goals are used to set direction. If you set a fitness goal and don't meet it, it's okay. Just do today more than you did yesterday. Enjoy the process, not the end result, because once you get there, you will just set a new goal anyway, and off you will go. Realize that if obtaining a certain goal takes longer than you expected, that may discourage you, and you may lose the motivation to exercise altogether. We don't want you to get discouraged.

I remember my grandfather wanted to get his biceps back. He lifted dumbbells every day for three weeks but did not see the improvement he anticipated. He became frustrated, and resultantly stopped working out altogether. I told him to work out, just to work out. We kept a little journal of the days he exercised, marking the ones when he did at least something with a colorful orange checkmark. He felt accomplished, and that feeling motivated him to keep going. He eventually got his biceps back.

Love the process, but do not forget about the progress. Some people set out goals to do one push-up more every day for ten years. In Philadelphia, a man did 3,655 non-stop push-ups in front of me, and I was offered the honor to count them. The current world record for the most push-ups done non-stop is 10,507, set by Minoru Yoshida of Japan in October 1980. [31]

How many push-ups do you think Minoru would be able to do when he is seventy? Consistency is key. This is a similar model for learning a one-finger push-up. I asked my friend who is a Shaolin monk, how does he do it? Turns out that you start by doing regular push-ups, then learn to do one-arm push-ups, and then start subtracting fingers from that hand. He said on average it takes about three years, but you have to train every day.

Some find this thrilling; some find it too repetitive. I encourage people to try new types of movement. Trying new physical activities promotes neurogenesis, and helps us stay active. Try what you have never done before. Maybe yoga, parkour, tai-chi, lay bike cycling, or anything else, no matter how old you are. Sometimes, even doing the same activity but at a new place also makes it more interesting and exciting.

The underlying belief that must accompany you is that a human body is limitless; the only limit is in your mind. With this belief comes great need for bodily awareness. With every year, you have to listen to your body more closely to avoid injury. No physical progress is worth an injury, because then you set yourself back.

Also, it is okay to take breaks. Just know that any break should not be too long, not only because it is easy to lose shape, but also because it is easy to unbuild a healthy habit. Inevitably, at some age, you'll reach a point where it will be more about maintaining your physical capabilities, rather than getting into better shape, and that is fine. When you get to that point, know that the time has come to try something you have never tried before.

I have been very fortunate to meet extraordinary people, who at an old age were able to do what most young people could not. It was inspiring. I met seventy-eight-year-old marathon runners, and a man who was able to do advanced gymnastics static elements at eighty-two. I was actually beat by a seventy-seven-year-old at a velodrome by a mile when I was twenty-six, and I have been cycling for years at that time. Every time I asked myself, "But, how?!" The formula is in the next few paragraphs.

---

[31] Wikipedia, "Push-up."

The key to physical advancement is to avoid plateauing. A plateau occurs when our body becomes used to the exercise and we no longer see results. This happens for two reasons.

First, it is if we do the same exercises. For the muscles to get used to the exercise, it takes about a month on average. If doing push-ups made you a lot stronger in the first week, doing the same push-ups on your fourth week will make very little difference. This can be countered by mixing up your exercises.

When I did personal training, I learned an effective technique called muscle confusion. It is when you work out the same body part using different exercises. Let's say you want stronger biceps. You find out all the bicep exercises. If you do all of them every day, you will plateau.

You can avoid that by doing one set of exercises on Monday, a second set of exercises on Tuesday, a third set on Wednesday, and on Thursday you go back to the set of exercises you did on Monday. After one to two months, switch out one of the exercises for a new, harder one. That way, your muscles will not be able to get used to the stress as easily, and you will continue seeing progress.

The second reason: we do not increase the intensity of the exercise. The intensity can be increased with making the exercise harder or doing more repetitions, depending on your goals. Seeing yourself get better, faster, stronger gives us a great feeling of accomplishment. As you recall, with a bigger feeling of accomplishment, more dopamine and serotonin are released, which gives us more motivation to push harder.

Merely staying in shape is great, but you do not really enjoy the beautiful progress, you just avoid a regress. So, if you do ten push-ups on Monday, do eleven push-ups on Tuesday. If you lift sixty pounds on Wednesday, lift sixty-five on Thursday. This will help you avoid plateauing as well. How do you think that guy who broke the world record for push-ups did it?

Lastly, train consciously. This one I completely neglected myself, up until recently, when I tore the ligaments in my left knee and had to do rehab. Many people just do reps and sets, getting the numbers in; they do it so they could say they did it. Very few people train with awareness of every single, little muscle and ligament involved in each exercise they do.

When you run, draw your attention to your toes, calves, knees, ankles, thighs, and back, and how they flex with every push, every landing. Really think about it. Where your attention goes, energy flows, so let that energy flow to the muscles that you need to do the workout. This promotes not just muscular stimulation, but also the neurological one, making the neurons fire more, and the muscles receive more oxygenation from an increased blood flow, which increases their performance. This applies to any physical exercise. This is how I rehabbed my knee, and avoided surgery.

I've met numerous people who were all about the gym, working out, cardio, and everything else, but their diet was nowhere near where it needed to be for them to harness the real results of their physical efforts. Many people want a six-pack, and they are willing to put the work in, but they are not willing to let go of those French fries, ice cream, and beer. Therefore, if I tell you about your physical advancement, I can't ignore the diet, as it is another aspect of your life that you have an amazing opportunity to advance.

Diet is another form of physical self-improvement, in my opinion. There is no such thing as an ultimate diet. We all have different lifestyles and different goals. Some want to lose weight; some want to gain it. Based on credible resources, I can tell you which foods give us energy, stimulate blood flow, and detox our bodies. The choice is yours, but you can always eat cleaner, better, and healthier.

Energy foods are those that are high in healthy fat. A ketogenic diet consists mostly of such fats, and includes but is not limited to foods such as: fish oil, organic butter, organic cheese, organic whipping cream, avocadoes, avocado oil, extra virgin olive oil, coconut milk/butter/oil/spread/flour, MCT oil, chia seeds, macadamia nut oil, ghee, almonds, full-fat yogurt.[32] So, why do those foods give us energy?

Triglycerides are a type of fat found in your blood. When we eat, our body converts any calories it does not need to use right away into

---

[32] Spritzler, "16 Foods to Eat on a Ketogenic Diet."

triglycerides.[33] Triglycerides are especially suited for energy storage because they pack more than twice as much energy as carbohydrates or proteins.[34] Foods listed above promote more triglycerides because they are high in fat. In addition, the cell's power plants, mitochondria, creates more of the body's main energy source called adenosine triphosphate, or ATP.[35] In a scientific study, when patients were put on the keto diet, the number of mitochondria in brain cells increased.[36] This means that healthy fats help us create more energy, and store more energy to use when we need it.

Foods that stimulate blood flow are important not only for athletes but for everyone, because with an increased blood flow, there is more blood going to all the muscles and organs. Our brain is one of them, so there is more oxygen-rich blood reaching it, which allows us to think faster, memorize more, and stay concentrated for longer. More importantly, such dietary choices help us avoid cardiovascular problems.

Those foods include: sardines, salmon, almond milk, tuna fish, cas or romaine lettuce, green leaf, sweet red peppers, mango, papaya, spinach, hazelnuts, avocado, beets, dark chocolate, oranges, and blueberries.[37] [38] [39] [40]

These foods stimulate blood flow in three ways. First, they reduce inflammation, which if unchecked leads to plaque buildup and narrowing of the arteries. [41] Second, they reduce blood viscosity, or how thick and sticky our blood is; blood should flow like red wine, not ketchup.

---

[33] Sumithran, et al., "Ketosis and appetite-mediating nutrients and hormones after weight loss." *European Journal of Clinical Nutrition,*
[34] Dutchen, "What Do Fats Do in the Body?"
[35] Bough, and Rho, "Anticonvulsant mechanisms of the ketogenic diet." *Epilepsia.*
[36] Siva, "Can ketogenic diet slow progression of ALS?" *Lancet Neurology.*
[37] Tavernise, "F.D.A. Sets 2018 Deadline to Rid Foods of Trans Fats." *New York Times.*
[38] Estruch, et al., "Primary Prevention of Cardiovascular Disease with a Mediterranean Diet." *New England Journal of Medicine.*
[39] Ding, et al., "Chocolate and Prevention of Cardiovascular Disease: A Systematic Review," *Nutrition & Metabolism* (London).
[40] Kromhout, et al., "Fish oil and omega 3 fatty acids in cardiovascular disease: do they really work?" *European Heart Journal.*
[41] Chan, et al., "A review of the cardiovascular benefits and antioxidant properties of allicin." *Phytotherapy Research.*

Third, they support healthy arterial function, making sure your arteries stay flexible and can dilate and contract as needed.[42]

Those three factors all help prevent cardiovascular problems, including high blood pressure and high heart rate. [43] A combination of the three ensures that all of the bodily functions are working at their full capacity, since every organ including the heart requires a healthy blood flow.

Notice that if you are doing everything right in all the chapters about the mind, but you are suffering from high blood pressure due to dietary reasons, then your body is still taking a toll. Thus, you are not living balanced. Meanwhile, it is hard to tap into our innate state of happiness when the majority of our attention is on solving health problems.

Foods that detox our body are crucial for our overall health. Our body is made up of four major systems: the endocrine or hormonal system, the immune system, the liver, and the gut. The collaboration and communication between those four parts is critical to its proper function. Toxins and hormone disruptors can interfere with the interaction between those systems. This can result in hormone imbalances, obesity, mental fog, memory loss, fatigue, lack of vitality, metabolic syndrome, and sleep disturbances.[44]

All of those also lower our vibrational frequencies, and it becomes harder to manifest that what you want. Our connection to the unified field of energy is the strongest when we have the most energy. When our connection is weak, it is much harder to make a powerful quantum event occur.

The liver is the detoxifier of the body. It is responsible for producing antioxidants that detoxify fat-soluble hormone disruptors; breaking down hormones like estrogen or insulin efficiently; and keeping cancer at bay. When we consume alcohol, drugs, medications, processed foods, junk food, fast food, foods with chemical additives and artificial flavorings, we increase the toxicity of the liver. When the liver is overwhelmed with toxins, it cannot produce the anti-oxidants at its full capacity. Consequently, estrogen or insulin levels begin to build up in the body. Fat-soluble toxins accumulate in fat, generating more fat. [45]

---

[42] The Franklin Institute. "Blood Vessels."
[43] Ludovici, et al., "Cocoa, blood pressure, and vascular function." *Frontiers in Nutrition.*
[44] Kumar, "The Importance of Detoxification for Health."
[45] Group, "10 Foods That Detox the Body." Global Healing.

This makes losing weight extremely difficult, even if we exercise and eat less, because the body cannot release the fat-soluble toxins. Therefore, to lose weight we have to eat foods that detoxify our liver. These foods include: lemon, sprouts, broccoli, kale, arugula, spinach, mung beans, barley, mint, coconut water, ashwagandha, red beets, turmeric, organic wheatgrass, horseradish tree leaf, moringa, spirulina, chlorella, matcha green tea, probiotic vegetable fiber from tapioca starch, ginger, luo han guo, goji berries, pomegranates seeds. [46] [47]

As you can see, it is all connected. When we take care of the body, we help the spirit and the mind. When we take care of the mind, we help the body and the spirit. When we take care of the spirit, we help the body and the mind. This is why we can't just ignore meditation, eating right, or understanding the tricks our mind plays on us. Now, let's move on to the most important part of this chapter, our sleep.

Sleep

My friend, this book is a representation of your perfect life. When we live balanced, we must know a little bit of everything, but master that which gives you the most joy, makes you the most money, and creates a difference in you and this world. That is the definition of a well-rounded person.

My Shaman, that I do astral projection training with, Rahgi, endlessly stressed the importance of sleep. He always said, "If we can generate movement from stillness, we can cultivate our energy body with no limits."

There are several books that are devoted to the study of sleep and how to get the most rest. The one I found the most useful is *Sleep Smarter* by Shawn Stevenson. It talks about how to fall into the fourth stage of sleep, which is where we get the most rest. According to the author, we should be done eating two hours before we go to sleep; we should not drink coffee eight hours before we go to sleep, because that is how long caffeine stays in our system; and that we should not look into a phone or

---

[46] Morse, The Detox Miracle Sourcebook: Raw Foods and Herbs for Complete Cellular Regeneration.
[47] Reid, The Tao of Detox: The Natural Way to Purify Your Body for Health and Longevity.

any screens before going to bed, due to them emitting ultraviolet lights that accelerate our neurotransmitters, which makes it harder for the brain to shut down when we go to bed. If we do have to use our screens right before bed, then Shawn suggests using UV glasses, which block the ultraviolet lights. [48]

Here are some other tips I compiled over the years, that can improve our sleep:

1. Room temperature: Get it cold! Use built-in AC or a "Bed Jet" if you're on a budget;

2. Get your room dark with blackout curtains;

3. Get it quiet with soundproof doors, sound deadening panels;

4. Optimize your room for a single purpose: Sleep (remove screens, clutter, desks, security, charge your phone on the opposite side of the room);

5. Light: Make sure you use tungsten bulbs, not fluorescent or LED mental asylum lights that irritate your nervous system;

6. Mattress and linens: harder mattress, linen or full-cotton sheets, goose down duvet inner, featherdown pillows (avoid synthetics);

7. Weighted blanket;

8. Circadian rhythms;

9. Make the winddown periods at least an hour.

Another factor that impacts our sleep, is how fast we fall asleep. This depends on how fast our brain can shut down and relax. A common problem is that because of our busy lives, many of us never really have a moment for ourselves. We are consonantly distracted by our phones, e-mails, work, or others. Resultantly, when we go to bed, it is often the first quiet moment we get all day, so we begin thinking, planning, imagining, or solving problems. This doesn't allow the brain to start resting.

To fix this, we have to consciously take time out of our day to be one-on-one with ourselves. This is when we can focus on our thoughts, feelings, and our reality. It is necessary to let our minds process what has

---

[48] Stevenson, *Sleep Smarter.*

been happening and how we have been feeling to avoid doing that when we go to bed. We can simply allocate some time during the day when we are not distracted by anything, even if it is just ten minutes.

Sleep is something we can improve infinitely. We can always fall asleep faster, and we can always go into deeper sleep where we experience lucid dreams. We can even start a dream journal and analyze our dreams, when we discover deeper sleep. The main goal is to feel better in the morning to perform better in the day.

Being in good physical shape is essential for not sabotaging our happiness. If we are suffering from health issues, it is very hard to derive joy from everything else. Also, since serving others or a cause greater than yourself is a big topic in our roadmap to a happier life, how much can you do for others if you cannot get yourself out of health problems? How much can a father support his family, if he cannot leave the hospital? People with serious health problems waste a large amount of their energy just on staying alive, instead of on experiences that bring them joy. This is why we have to be in the best shape we can be to live a happier life.

Conclusion

I'm not a fan of long conclusions. This is the end, my friend, and any end should be quick, just like a goodbye. It makes it less painful that way. You have no idea how much I enjoyed telling you all of these stories and lessons, and so I thank you. Remember, to give more, we have to be more.

It all begins with our attention. If we can control it, we can control our lives, and eventually, we can control the physical world around us. Sometimes, all we have to do is just change our perspective, and see THE OTHER SIDE. Now spread the word, my friend, the power is within you.

Here is a summary of our main principles:

Have no doubt

The Universe is perfect

How can I serve?

See the world in oneness

See your emotions in oneness

Negative self-talk will never help you, besides you're not always right

Happiness is in the movement, not the destination

The divine power of will is within you

Goals are set to create direction

If there is a possibility, believe in it

Acknowledgments

My Publisher

Book cover art design by Asel Sadekova https://www.aseldesigns.com/

About the Author

Dan Ginzburg has been doing general life coaching since 2015, before becoming a lawyer. However, he began working on this book far before then. Dan has used material from this book to speak at several law firms, events, schools and universities about mindfulness and conscious leadership. Also in 2015, Dan became the founder of Human Social Movement, which is a platform for like-minded spiritual individuals to share their knowledge with others who are open to spirituality. Through Human Social Movement, Dan holds monthly group meditations in Los Angeles.

More recently, Dan became a consultant for attorneys, specializing in scaling attorneys' law practices. Yet not only does Dan help lawyers become more profitable, he also guides them in becoming more organized, productive, motivated, and less stressed. As a lawyer, Dan has firsthand experience with attorneys' struggles. This is why he has dedicated himself to giving lawyers the tools to not only increase their profits, but also their happiness.

Dan believes in the importance of living for a cause that is greater than yourself. For Dan, that cause is uniting people through spirituality with Human Social Movement and helping attorneys find life balance in one of the most chaotic professions there is through his program "More Money, Less Stress, Better You."

During the 2020 pandemic, Dan's life took a sudden, unexpected turn. During mass shutdowns and people losing not only work, but hope, Dan knew he had to create something that would pull people out of their distressed states. With this in mind, Double Reality Gallery in Los Angeles was born. What Dan didn't know is that he had inadvertently created the world's first virtual/augmented reality gallery. The gallery not only offered an incomparably unique visual experience, but incorporated spiritual messages and key lessons from this book in each and every tour.

Dan also believes that meditation, mindfulness and a strong power of will are among some of the most important things for improving one's life. However, Dan's bigger goal is to live by what he teaches and that is to be a well-rounded person himself. He strives not only to be the messenger, but to be THE message.

Website: www.hsmovement.com

Email: Ginzburg@hsmovement.com

Instagram: https://www.instagram.com/danginzburg_/

References

Amorim, Josane Mary. "The heart is 5000 times stronger magnetically than the brain!" Josane Mary blog. May 6, 2016. Retrieved from https://josanemary.wordpress.com/2016/05/06/the-heart-is-5000-times-stronger-magnetically-than-the-brain/

Bailey, Frazer, (director). E-Motion 2.0, Justin Lyons (producer), Warren, NJ: Passion River Productions, 2014.

Bergland, Christopher. "The Neurochemicals of Happiness," Psychology Today blog, November 29, 2012. (from The Athlete's Way)

Bhatt, Deepak. "'Stress' cardiomyopathy: A different kind of heart attack," Harvard Health Blog, September 03, 2015. Retrieved from https://www.health.harvard.edu/blog/stress-cardiomyopathy-a-different-kind-of-heart-attack-201509038239

Black, Paul H., and Garbutt, Lisa D. "Stress, inflammation and cardiovascular disease," (Abstract), National Library of Medicine, January 2002. Retrieved from https://www.ncbi.nlm.nih.gov/pubmed/11801260

Bough, K.J., and Rho, J.M. "Anticonvulsant mechanisms of the ketogenic diet." Epilepsia, 2007; 48: 43–58.

Brookshire, Bethany. "Explainer: What is dopamine?" Science News for Students, January 17, 2017. Retrieved from https://www.sciencenewsforstudents.org/article/explainer-what-dopamine

Chan, Jackie Yan-Yan; Yuen, Ailsa Chui-Ying; Chan, Robbie Yat-Kan; Chan, Shun-Wan. "A review of the cardiovascular benefits and antioxidant properties of allicin." Phytotherapy Research. 2013 May;27(5):637–46.

Ding, Eric L.; Hutfless, Susan M.; Ding, Xin; Girotra, Saket. "Chocolate and Prevention of Cardiovascular Disease: A Systematic Review," Nutrition & Metabolism (London). 2006; 3:2.

Dispenza, Joe. Becoming Supernatural. Carlsbad, CA: Hay House, Inc., 2017

Dispenza, Joe. Becoming Supernatural: How Common People Are Doing the Uncommon. Audiobook, Carlsbad, CA: Hay House, Inc., June 2018

Dutchen, Stephanie. "What Do Fats Do in the Body?" LiveScience. (no date) Retrieved from https://www.livescience.com/9109-fats-body.html

Estruch, R., et al. "Primary Prevention of Cardiovascular Disease with a Mediterranean Diet." New England Journal of Medicine, 2013; 368:1279-1290

Flint Rehab, and Maher, Courtney. "Can Stress Cause a Stroke? What You Need to Know", Neurological Recovery Blog, updated August 26, 2020. Retrieved from https://www.flintrehab.com/2015/can-stress-cause-a-stroke/

The Franklin Institute. "Blood Vessels". Accessed January 7, 2018. Retrieved from https://www.fi.edu/heart/blood-vessels

Group, Edward. "10 Foods That Detox the Body." Global Healing. Updated March 14, 2017. Retrieved from https://globalhealing.com/natural-health/foods-that-detox-the-body/

Hanson, Rick. "Confronting the Negativity Bias," 2018. Retrieved from https://dev.rickhanson.net/how-your-brain-makes-you-easily-intimidated

Kromhout, Daan; Yasuda, Satoshi; Geleijnse, Johanna M.; Shimokawa, Hiroaki. "Fish oil and omega 3 fatty acids in cardiovascular disease: do they really work?" European Heart Journal. 2012 Feb; 33(4): 436–443.

Kumar, Rose. "The Importance of Detoxification for Health." Huffington Post. March 4, 2016, updated March 5, 2017. Retrieved from https://www.huffingtonpost.com/rose-kumar-md/the-importance-of-detoxif_b_9379300.html

Lambdin, Thomas O. (translator). The Gospel of Thomas. Retrieved from https://www.marquette.edu/maqom/Gospel%20of%20Thomas%20Lambdin.pdf

Loehr, Jim, The Only Way to Win. New York: Hyperion Books, 2012

Ludovici, Valeria; Barthelmes, Jens; Näjele, Matthias P.; Enseleit, Frank; Ferri, Claudio; Flammer, Andreas J.; Ruschitzka, Frank; and Sudano, Isabella. "Cocoa, blood pressure, and vascular function." Frontiers in Nutrition. 2017; 4:36.

Morse, R., The Detox Miracle Sourcebook: Raw Foods and Herbs for Complete Cellular Regeneration, Kalindi Press, 2013

Munn, Stephanie. "Does stress cause skin problems?" All Healthy Me articles, January 20, 2017. Retrieved from https://www.bupa.co.uk/newsroom/ourviews/does-stress-cause-skin-problems

National Headache Foundation. "Stress" News blog, Oct. 25, 2007. Retrieved from https://headaches.org/2007/10/25/stress/

National Kidney Foundation, "Stress and Your Kidneys" New York. June 5, 2020. Retrieved from https://www.kidney.org/atoz/content/Stress_and_your_Kidneys

Reid, D., The Tao of Detox: The Natural Way to Purify Your Body for Health and Longevity, Simon & Schuster UK, 2016

Rein, Glen, and McCraty, Rollin. "Structural Changes in Water and DNA Associated with New Philosophically Measurable States," Journal of Scientific Exploration, vol 8, no 3 (1994).

Runwonder (pseud.). "2018 Science Explains What Happens to Someone's Brain From Complaining Every Day." Runwonder.org. Accessed April 30, 2021. Retrieved from http://www.balancedweightmanagement.com/2018%20Science%20Explains%20What%20Happens%20to%20Someone.pdf

ScienceBlog. "Happiness: A Theory–Jaak Panksepp And The Seeking System," January 18, 2010. Retrieved from https://scienceblog.com/29222/happiness-a-theory-jaak-panksepp-and-the-seeking-system/

Silvertooth, E.W. "Special Relativity," Nature, Vol 322 (August 1986).

Siva, N. "Can ketogenic diet slow progression of ALS?" Lancet Neurology, 2006; 5: 476.

Spritzler, Franzika. "16 Foods to Eat on a Ketogenic Diet." HealthLine. Updated October 16, 2020. Retrieved from https://www.healthline.com/nutrition/ketogenic-diet-foods

Stuewer, Roger H. "Max Planck." Britannica, www.britannica.org. Updated April 19, 2021. Retrieved from https://www.britannica.com/biography/Max-Planck

Stevenson, Shawn. Sleep Smarter: 21 Essential Strategies to Sleep Your Way to A Better Body, Better Health, and Bigger Success. Emmaus, PA: Rodale Books. 2016

Sumithran, P., Prendergast, L.A., Delbridge, E., Purcell, K., Shulkes, A., Kriketos, A., and Proietto, J. "Ketosis and appetite-mediating nutrients and hormones after weight loss." European Journal of Clinical Nutrition, 2013; e-pub ahead of print 1 May 2013; doi:10.1038/ejcn.2013.90.

Tavernise, S., "F.D.A. Sets 2018 Deadline to Rid Foods of Trans Fats." New York Times. 16 Jun 2015. Accessed January 8, 2018

Weaver, David R., and Reppert, Steven M. "Definition of the developmental transition from dopaminergic to photic regulation of c-fos gene expression in the rat suprachiasmatic nucleus," Molecular Brain Research, Volume 33, Issue 1, October 1995, pp. 136-148

Wikipedia. "Aether theories." Retrieved from https://en.wikipedia.org/wiki/Aether_theories

———. "Michelson-Morley experiment." Retrieved from https://simple.wikipedia.org/wiki/Michelson–Morley_experiment

———. "Push-up." Retrieved from https://en.wikipedia.org/wiki/Push-up

Willink, Jocko, and Babin, Leif. Extreme Ownership: How U.S. Navy SEALs Lead and Win. Sydney: Macmillan Australia, 2018

Willis, M.A., and Haines, D.E. "The Limbic System." ScienceDirect. 2018, Retrieved from https://www.sciencedirect.com/topics/neuroscience/nucleus-accumbens

Yale News, "Stress Triggers Tumor Formation, Yale Researchers Find", January 13, 2010. Retrieved from https://news.yale.edu/2010/01/13/stress-triggers-tumor-formation-yale-researchers-find

Zweig, Jason. "Your money and your brain." August 23, 2007. Retrieved from http://stanford.edu/group/spanlab/Press/bk082307press.html

Reviews

Dan Ginzburg's book, *The Other Side*, is filled with great wisdom accrued through stories from enlightened beings as well as his own personal experience. What stands out to me is the practicality of his words. Dan is a straightforward writer, which makes his offer of spiritual insight applicable and doable. He also drives home the point that we are spiritual beings first and foremost, the rest is temporary at best. Dan has many nuggets of wisdom in his book and he walks gracefully hand-in-hand with the reader as he presents them. You will love his book.

– Jean Walters, best-selling author
www.Spiritualtransformation.com

As a holistic healer from birth, it was overwhelming and exciting to read this amazing guide toward understanding, self-development and evolution. Dan deeply described ways to gain true balance and connection with oneself, the universe, our communities, families, and more. He demonstrates respect and honor for the wisdom he received in his journey and goes even further by sharing the steps he took to achieve his own success. The deep meaning of transcending, integrating, and evolving is the need to help others achieve it in collaboration. Expansion and conscious mastery start on the first page of this book!

–Maricruz P. Ibarra, B.A. psychology, founder &
CEO of Energy Sync Wellness
www.energysyncwellness.com

Dan Ginzburg's *The Other Side* is so fulfilling I could not put it down. His writing is very easy to understand and flows nicely. I have gained a lot of insight which is going to help me in my continued personal and spiritual growth. Dan gives us many ways to overcome stress and life situations to break down so many barriers that we put upon ourselves. I have been through many of these situations and Dan's insights put it all into perspective. I highly recommend this book to anyone looking to be eternally happy, independently of anything or anyone. To echo Dan's words, "Why not be limitless?" This book teaches you how and by following Dan's writing, I will become limitless and stay happy. Thank you, Dan!

– Catherine Laub, keynote speaker, author, podcaster,
The Elite Turquoise Mentor Program
www.thetqlady.com

Let's Continue Our Relationship!

We would love to connect with you and go deeper. Listed below, please see the top three ways you can connect with us and continue your experience to the other side. We hope you lean in to one of the opportunities listed below. We look forward to staying connected and to support you on your journey.

Group Meditations

Join us to watch a sunset on the beach, meditate with other amazing human beings and rise to higher vibrations together!

Scan me!

Or follow the link below

https://www.meetup.com/Santa-Monica-Sunset-Meditation-Group/

Penthouse Augmented Reality Gallery Experience with Wine Tasting

Grab your +1 and submerge yourself into 2 hours of the most imagination expanding visual experience of your life!

Scan me!

Or follow the link below

https://www.eventbrite.com/e/132334894231

Course

A condensed version of this book that personally guides you through the most critical points to help you achieve a balanced life and manifest your dreams and desires. The course includes videos, pictures, diagrams and worksheets for you to use to light up the path to your bright, beautiful, new future.

Scan me!

Or follow the link below

https://danginzburg.thinkific.com/courses/
more-money-less-stress-better-you

Lightning Source UK Ltd.
Milton Keynes UK
UKHW022130160921
390713UK00002B/364